Practicing Sociology
in the Community

Practicing Sociology in the Community

A Student's Guide

Phyllis Ann Langton

George Washington University

Dianne Anderson Kammerer

Kammerer Consulting Group

PEARSON

Prentice
Hall

Upper Saddle River, New Jersey 07458

Library of Congress Cataloging-in-Publication Data

Langton, Phyllis Ann.
    Practicing sociology in the community: a student's guide/Phyllis Ann Langton, Dianne Anderson Kammerer.
        p. cm.
    Includes bibliographical references and index.
    ISBN 0-13-042019-0
    1. Applied sociology.   2. Sociology—Research.   3. Community.
I. Kammerer, Dianne Anderson.   II. Title.

HN29.5.L36 2004
301—dc22   2004014152

AVP, Publisher: Nancy Roberts
Executive Editor: Christopher DeJohn
Editorial Assistant: Kristin Haegele
Marketing Manager: Marissa Feliberty
Prepress and Manufacturing Buyer: Mary Ann Gloriande
Interior Design: John P. Mazzola
Cover Design: Bruce Kenselaar
Composition/Full-Service Project Management: Kari Callaghan Mazzola and John P. Mazzola
Printer/Binder: Von Hoffmann
Cover Printer: Coral Graphics

This book was set in 10/12 New Century Schoolbook.

Pearson Education LTD.
Pearson Education Singapore, Pte. Ltd
Pearson Education, Canada, Ltd
Pearson Education–Japan
Pearson Education Australia PTY, Limited

Pearson Education North Asia Ltd
Pearson Educación de Mexico, S.A. de C.V.
Pearson Education Malaysia, Pte. Ltd
Pearson Education, Upper Saddle River, NJ

10 9 8 7 6 5 4 3 2 1
ISBN 0-13-042019-0

For Claire and Lorna Ramage, Adrian, Colin, and Genevieve Lamoureux,
a new generation of social activists

Contents

Preface

We wrote this guide for all students who are fortunate enough to practice sociology in the community. We speak to you through stories, our experiences, the experiences of students we have known, and sociological theories and research that help inform this process of bridging the university and the community.

We have addressed six objectives in this guide:

- To provide an overview of what it means to practice sociology
- To challenge you to use a critical approach and to develop and apply critical thinking skills
- To demonstrate the importance of keeping a journal and doing systematic observation and research
- To engage you in the process of bridging the classroom and the community
- To encourage you to think about social justice, and act when possible to reduce inequalities in society
- To offer you specific strategies for reflection

This guide is designed as a supplement to the text or readings provided for your course in community-based learning. It is organized to facilitate your ability to connect what you learn in the classroom with your experiences in the community—and further, to take your experiences in the community back to the classroom, reflecting upon what these experiences mean for you, for the community, and for the development of sociological knowledge. It is our purpose to illustrate ways of practicing sociology in the community that are meaningful for advancing your sociological understanding as well as making a difference in the community and your personal life.

Practicing sociology in the community is an important life-shaping process. We have tried to prepare you for the experience by raising issues throughout this guide that you may encounter in the community as well as in your classroom. We encourage you to use a critical approach and to develop critical thinking skills that will help you move beyond your own experiences.

ACKNOWLEDGMENTS

Many people and events shaped our writing of this guide. First, we thank all of our students for stimulating us to think about the aspects of practicing sociology that are important to them. Thanks also go to our students April Dreeke, Kipp Efinger, and Kerrie Watkins for the journal entries they permitted us to quote in this guide. We thank our colleagues Professors Walda Katz-Fishman and Sam Marullo for their very generous sharing of their stories about becoming social activists. We are also grateful to George Thomas, Bernice Hawkey, and Ona Kammerer, who, during the most difficult times of their serious illnesses, encouraged us to continue with our writing.

We relied on the advice and encouragement of Christopher DeJohn, Executive Editor for Sociology at Prentice Hall, who made us rewrite many drafts. Kari Callaghan Mazzola of Big Sky Composition applied her expertise to prepare and produce this guide. We thank both Chris and Kari for their generous efforts. We also thank the following reviewers, who gave helpful suggestions during the manuscript stage: Sara Horsfall of Texas Wesleyan University, Ronald Elliott Hughes of California State University–Fullerton, Lynda James of SUNY–Plattsburgh, J. Richard Kenrick, Jr., of SUNY–Cortland, Ginger Macheski of Valdosta State University, Roseanne Martorella of William Paterson University, and Dan Neuss of University of Wisconsin. Finally, this experience has been possible because of the respect, love, and laughter shared by the authors.

Phyllis Ann Langton
Dianne Anderson Kammerer

Practicing Sociology
in the Community

CHAPTER 1

Introduction

We have written *Practicing Sociology in the Community: A Student's Guide* for you to use during your community-based learning program. While we speak to various community-based learning programs in this guide, our primary focus is on service-learning and service-learning advocacy, and less on internships. Generally, the former two programs place emphasis on integrating your community experiences with your educational experiences through opportunities for reflection in the classroom, instead of primarily acquiring preprofessional experience as in many internship programs. In addition, doing service-learning advocacy directs your attention to issues of social justice. We want you to learn how to connect social issues and social justice and how these can become a central focus of community-based learning.

All of us are shaped by our own experiences and history, therefore we identify some basic assumptions that have affected our thinking and that we build upon in writing this guide for you.

- You benefit from taking responsibility for your learning by being an active and self-motivated learner.
- You enhance your knowledge by integrating your academic study with community participation.

- You develop your sociological imagination by using critical thinking.
- You learn by confronting new situations with curiosity, opening up your mind to new perspectives.
- You create a basis for pursing social justice by using a critical sociological approach and engaging in social change.

We are preparing you to question existing social arrangements in a community and to reflect on why things are the way they are. One way to start questioning is by turning to the ways society is structured. Throughout this guide we suggest that looking at individual characteristics cannot provide an understanding of why some groups in society are poor, while others are stigmatized because of their sexual orientation, or why others have limited control over what goes on in their lives because of their gender or age. Mark Chesler puts it this way:

> [Community service-learning combined with] sociological information and analytic frameworks can help students "look upstream" and identify the structural and institutional sources of the individual and social problems they encounter. (1993, 1)

Structural arrangements in society that create social problems such as poverty, violence, hunger, or hate crimes are not a consequence of individuals and their personalities. When more than a few people are living in poverty, one should look for forces outside individuals, rather than look at their personal faults, to see why this is so. For example, people are often not paid adequate wages for their work, which causes them to live in poverty.

In this chapter we introduce you to what we mean by practicing sociology. We want you to start reflecting upon your own knowledge of sociological practice and how it can help you learn in your community-based program. Next, we introduce you to one way of conceptualizing community-based learning programs. After reading this section, you may want to discuss with your faculty advisor the various definitions of community-based learning programs that you have read about or learned in the classroom. Discussing the various types of programs can help you make an informed decision about what other programs you might want to consider. You may decide you are more interested in service-learning advocacy while someone else may want to select an internship program. Next, we introduce you to the idea of social justice. We include in this section definitions of social justice, moving from a model of charity to one of social justice, and conversations with two scholar activists. Their stories provide a glimpse of the strategies that they have used to bridge the university and the community in the pursuit of social justice. Their stories also illustrate how faculty members work with students and community members.

PRACTICING SOCIOLOGY

Practicing sociology is both a way of thinking and a process that you undertake to help you understand the social world in which you live. In this section, we begin with a brief overview of practicing sociology. Practicing sociology also includes the processes of critical thinking and critical reflection. Both of these processes are important for you to understand and apply when practicing sociology in a community, as well as in your personal lives. We conclude this section by introducing you to what we mean by a critical sociological approach.

OVERVIEW

When you are **practicing sociology** you are engaging in a particular way of thinking and doing that allows you to understand how individuals are active participants in shaping their social world. Your actions and life are organized by your relationships with others, meaning that they are structured and not merely random events (Shaw 1997). Through your actions, you reproduce or change social structure over time. Think about your college experiences. Although your experiences are not exactly the same as all other college students, there are some patterns. You are expected to attend most classes that are generally held in classrooms. The professor is expected to organize what is covered in the classroom. You are expected to take the role of student to learn and gain knowledge.

Driving an automobile provides you with another example of structure. Reflect on your driving experiences. In the United States, you must be at a legal age to drive, and this age varies by state laws. You must have a learner's permit or driver's license. You must drive on the right side of the road. These examples illustrate what we mean by social structure. If you choose to resist this structure by driving in other ways, your behavior may be challenged by irate motorists cursing at you, or, in the worst of circumstances, you could be involved in a serious accident. These examples also illustrate how you are making choices that are shaped by your culture. If you lived in Ireland, the norm would be to drive on the left side of the road. If you lived in Japan and you were sixteen, you would be below the legal age to drive a car.

Viewing your experiences in the community through a sociological lens that focuses your attention on structural issues also provides you with an opportunity to be an advocate for social justice. **Advocacy** is a political process of changing social arrangements (social structure) that are already acceptable for some people (Eyler and Giles 1999, 131). For example, if you were doing a service-learning advocacy program, you might be helping with a needs assessment study for a community attempting to create more housing for the poor. You might also use your research skills to help an advocacy group who is working with a legislator to draft a bill regarding medical use of marijuana for AIDS patients.

Not all of you have been politically active in the past, but when you practice sociology with an orientation toward social justice you have an opportunity to learn about social advocacy. We believe that you should be exposed to social advocacy and social justice issues as part of your university experience. We are not alone in our belief that practicing sociology in the community and the pursuit of justice are important aspects of a sociological education. In 2000 and 2003, the Society for the Study of Social Problems (SSSP), one of several professional associations that sociologists support, also emphasized social justice as a component of academic sociology.

In summary, Chesler (1993, 1) notes that there are three general questions that are important to ask and answer in a community-based learning program. Question one "involves seeing and participating in WHAT [capitalization in text] is happening." Question two "involves seeing and understanding HOW things happen." Question three "involves asking and answering WHY things happen the way they do." Asking and answering these questions will focus your attention on structural sources for situations. Also, these questions are important ways of uncovering information through critical thinking.

CRITICAL THINKING

Critical thinking is an essential part of your sociological education as well as of your community-based learning program. Critical thinking is likely to make you more engaged in your learning and provides you with the context for identifying existing social problems and exploring alternative ways of thinking about and acting on these problems (Bean 1996). Sam Marullo (1999, 15), a sociologist, notes that you will improve your critical thinking in the field because you are forced to confront simplistic and individualistic explanations of social problems you observe in a community or organization. He argues that bringing together readings, class discussion, faculty-student dialogue, and interactions with people in the field forces you to see the structural and institutional factors that shape issues in the field.

Throughout your community-based learning program you will be challenged to expand your thinking about the experiences you have in a community or organization. This guide provides you with some ideas of how to do this. To illustrate: Reading on a topic of interest to you may bring some surprises and opportunities for you to reflect and wonder. For example, what is your reaction when you read the following passage from *The Forgotten Americans?*

> Americans have always believed that in a free society people showing individual responsibility and diligence will get ahead. So deeply ingrained is this belief that it is known as the American ethos. Yet each day millions of responsible Americans return home from their jobs to lives of enduring economic struggle. All of them are employed full-time the entire year and conscientiously practice the work ethic. Despite their hard work, they live in poverty. (Schwarz and Volgy 1992, 3)

For many of you, poverty means being without employment but these people described above are what we call the **working poor.** Studies show that the failure of hard work to provide a minimal decent return transcends the boundaries of race or gender, and even of workers' educational credentials. White males make up the largest group of employed heads of household who live in poverty (1992, 5). So what does this tell you that you did not know? We provide you with "mental habits" in Chapter 2 to help answer this question. Critical thinking helps develop mental habits and creates processes that are necessary for practicing sociology. These mental habits and processes include critical listening, questioning, reading, observing, analyzing, and writing.

Critical thinking takes practice and time, but you can learn how to do it. At times you may find yourself willing to settle for your own personal opinion rather than using critical thinking. Try to avoid this! We hope that once you have learned critical thinking you will make it an integral part of your personal life as well as a continuing part of your educational experience.

CRITICAL REFLECTION

Along with critical thinking, **critical reflection,** where you explore your own assumptions about social life and how it is organized, is also important when you practice sociology. It provides you with the ability to think critically and to reflect upon these experiences guided by sociological insights often derived from your coursework or readings. You may experience some discomfort in this process as your reflection exposes some truths about your character and your feelings. For example, some of you may have to confront your own sexist or homophobic behaviors. This is a dialectical process whereby you develop meaning through the interplay of your community experiences with your course material. It also calls into use critical thinking, discussed earlier in the guide.

With critical reflection you become an active learner, that is, you learn not merely by doing but by thinking and reflecting about what you are doing. You are challenged to consider your own assumptions and biases in light of the evidence that you discover in a community. This may mean challenging unjust social structures or oppressive institutional arrangements within an agency in addition to sometimes changing your own personal beliefs.

There are many ways to develop your ability to reflect. You may be asked to write papers, work in groups within the classroom, speak to your class members or to people in the community, or listen to others.

Finally, there appear to be several benefits when you engage in reflection.

- Reflection transforms experience into genuine learning about individual values and goals and about larger social issues.
- Reflection challenges students to connect service activities to course objectives and to develop higher-level thinking and problem solving.
- Reflection works against the perpetuation of stereotypes by raising students' awareness of structures surrounding service environments.
- By fostering a sense of connection to the community and a deeper awareness of community needs, reflection increases the likelihood that students will remain committed to service beyond the term of the course. (Colorado State University 1997–2003, 1)

Read this list carefully. Throughout your community-based learning program, review the list and ask yourself: "Do I agree with the statements on this list?" "Is there evidence to support these ideas?" "Do I have other benefits that I can add to this list?" Write down the answers to these questions in your journal, discussed in Chapter 4.

A CRITICAL SOCIOLOGICAL APPROACH

As you read this guide, you will see that we take a critical sociological approach to understanding everyday life in the United States. A **critical sociological approach** means that sociology is useful for identifying what social conditions can and should be changed and how people can go about changing them (Neubeck and Glasberg 1996). Community-based learning programs that engage you in field research in the pursuit of social justice are most likely to provide you with continuous opportunities for using a critical sociological approach.

Using a critical sociological approach involves asking questions, such as: "What do structures of injustice in this society mean for different social groups?" For example, one consequence of the structure of the U.S. economic system is an increasing disparity between the incomes of the rich and those of the poor. To explore why this is so you need to look at those groups who have privilege in this society, who have the power to maintain the status quo, and who perpetuate systems of injustice in this society. A critical sociological approach also looks to the oppressed people in society who, no matter how hard they try, cannot participate in life to its fullest.

The sociologist Randall Collins (1998) notes that many students come to sociology with a belief in helping those who struggle to find fulfilling lives. When you practice sociology in the pursuit of social justice, you analyze social problems as structural issues and actively use these data to effect social change. You and the community benefit under these conditions. The benefit is linked to the idea that "Being sociologically mindful is a way to see how what we become as people depends on the nature of our ties to others" (Schwalbe 2001, 64). For example, the concept of **sociological mindfulness** leads you to pay attention to what is around you and to consider alternative explanations to the taken-for-granted myths (Schwalbe 2001).

In the next section, we introduce you to practicing sociology in a community-based learning program. We begin with a discussion of three types of community-based learning: internships, service-learning, and service-learning advocacy.

COMMUNITY-BASED LEARNING

There are various opportunities for you to practice sociology through community-based learning programs in colleges and universities. **Community-based learning** "is a dimension of educating students in an academic discipline while also preparing them to be contributing citizens" (Portland State University). Options for programs within community-based learning are often given different names, depending upon where these are located in the university structure and the degree to which classroom work informs learning. Two sociologists identify six options for community-based learning. These include the following:

- Out-of-class activities (example: field trips, no credit)
- Volunteering (example: helping homeless women find appropriate clothing, no credit)
- Service add-ons (example: earning additional credit for volunteering)
- Internships (example: preprofessional experience working in a lawyer's office and receiving credit)
- Service-learning (example: participating as an advocate for children in a community as part of the juvenile justice system, reflecting on these experiences to further understand course material, critical reflection and receiving credit)
- Service-learning advocacy (example: lobbying city government for better public housing, which requires reflection, and challenging unjust structural arrangements, and receiving credit) (Mooney and Edwards 2001, 184)

Linda Mooney and Bob Edwards (2001) distinguish several essential components of each of these community models: service, curricular credit, apply/acquire skills, structured reflection, and social action.

INTERNSHIPS

Within your sociology department, you are more likely to be offered an internship program than service-learning or service-advocacy programs. Marianne Green (1997, 16) observes that internship programs tend to build firm bridges between the university and the community. This occurs when there is cross-fertilization of ideas and resources. However, how colleges and universities define and conduct internship programs differ widely. Thus, there is not uniformity on how internship programs are structured into university programs, as there is not agreement as to the academic value of integrating classroom and community learning.

In our review, we found large variations among sociology departments on the availability of internships, whether it is required for the major or an elective, and whether it is taught in the sociology department. We find that when the course is located in the major department, you are more likely to interact with your faculty director than when it is located outside the sociology department in the college. Such interaction is likely to increase the degree of integration of theoretical and experiential knowledge that is at the heart of doing an internship experience in an academic program. Susan Chizeck (1999, 41) argues, "An internship without substantial faculty involvement becomes only career exploration devoid of academic content."

Mooney and Edwards (2001, 185) categorize internships as practica, cooperative learning or field placements that are pre-professional experiences often offered as stand-alone courses. They find that structured reflection is often not required for internships, as it is in service-learning and service-learning advocacy. The American Sociological Association (ASA) informs us that in 1999 about half of the 2,200 departments of sociology and related disciplines had internship courses for their students.

SERVICE-LEARNING

Like internship programs, there are many definitions and models of service-learning programs. For example, Janet Eyler and Dwight Giles (1999) report that in 1990 there were 147 definitions of such programs. Consequently, there are many different types of programs (Hironimus-Wendt and Lovell-Troy 1999; Mooney and Edwards 2001). There is a vast literature on this topic. We found fewer sociologists writing on this pedagogy than other educators (Potter et al. 2003).

According to the Corporation for National and Community Service, service-learning does the following:

- Promotes learning through active participation in service experiences
- Provides structured time for students to reflect by thinking, discussing and/or writing about their service experience
- Provides an opportunity for students to use skills and knowledge in real-life situations
- Extends learning beyond the classroom and into the community
- Fosters a sense of caring for others (adapted from the National and Community Service Act of 1990 by National Service-Learning Clearinghouse 1994)

The article does suggest that although there are many different meanings of service-learning, there appears to be "a core concept" that most people agree with.

> Service-learning combines service objectives with learning objectives with the intent that the activity change both the recipient and the provider of the service. This is accomplished by combining service tasks with structured opportunities that link the task to self-reflection, self-discovery, and the acquisition and comprehension of values, skills, and knowledge content. (National Service-Learning Clearinghouse 1994)

The impetus for service-learning in sociology is grounded in the works of John Dewey, a philosopher and educator, and the sociologist C. Wright Mills, the latter building on the work of Dewey. Why is sociology a candidate for service-learning? There are at least three reasons:

1. It fits into a long tradition of activist community sociology.
2. To the degree that we validate experience as one among many sources of knowledge, service-learning provides an additional way to educate students.
3. It furthers the goals of social justice and the development of our students into citizen-scholars. (Hironimus-Wendt and Lovell-Troy 1999)

That service-learning is a good "fit" with sociology seems clear. Yet, at the time of this writing, there are fewer service-learning programs than internship programs in sociology. Internships often focus on pre-professional experience.

Service-learning provides the opportunity to learn through connecting classroom knowledge with experiences in the field. The essential components of this learning include applying and acquiring skills and structured reflection, which requires the integration of both individual and group processes (Mooney and Edwards 2001, 186).

SERVICE-LEARNING ADVOCACY

Service-learning advocacy shares similarities with service-learning. A key difference is that service-learning advocacy frames the idea of service in terms of social justice. Thus, if you participate in a service-learning advocacy program, it is likely that you will be expected to become an advocate for social change. Sometimes students are reticent about confronting inequalities that are identified in a community or organization. This is not unusual, especially if you have not been involved in some type of advocacy work. However, you have many sources available to you that can at least help minimize your discomfort, including bringing your feelings and emotions into the classroom to share with others.

Here are some of the potential benefits of service-learning advocacy according to Mooney and Edwards (2001, 189).

- Enhance citizen education/civic literacy
- Develop and hone leadership skills
- Act as an agent of social change
- Gain experiential knowledge of power relations
- Enhance political socialization
- Become empowered
- Enhance moral character development
- Gain collaborative skills
- Adopt an interdisciplinary approach

For example, you may develop leadership skills that you can use to promote social change. You may become a citizen leader by becoming involved in civic arrangements and working with stakeholders to enact social change. Or you may become active on campus by setting up groups to address diversity and political action. Our students have been successful at setting up political action groups on campus and forming partnerships with other organizations to provide services for women, including students, who have been abused.

Mooney and Edwards summarize clearly the service-learning advocacy agenda:

> A key pedagogical enhancement of service-learning advocacy owes to its explicit social change agenda the assumption that people begin to appreciate fully the relations of power in a society as they endeavor to affect social change in the context of critical reflection and dialogue with others who are similarly engaged. (2001, 187)

We share a focus with Marullo and Edwards who are committed to service-learning advocacy and social justice. The questions they pose about the teaching and learning process should highlight for you many of the issues and concerns of service-learning advocacy:

1. Does the community service work undertaken by students in their service-learning classes empower the recipients?
2. Are students required to examine whether and how their service work helps to address the root causes of the problem?
3. Does the service-learning encourage students to see that the shortcomings of individuals in need are not the sole cause of the problems that service-learning activities attempt to address?
4. Are the institutional operations of the university-community partnerships organized in such a way as to support and sustain the collaborative efforts of faculty, students, and community members?
5. Does the university-community collaboration build community, increase social capital, and enhance diversity?
6. Do educational institutions operate their community partnership programs in accord with social justice principles? (Marullo and Edwards 2000, 901–910)

Marullo and Edwards argue for an educational system that provides opportunities for students to participate in the vision of transforming society from a focus on charity to a commitment to social justice. Underlying these questions is the assumption that it is important to decrease inequality and the harmful effects of poverty.

Joe Feagin and Hernan Vera in *Liberation Sociology* (2001) show that sociology can make a vital contribution to human freedom and well-being. They provide careful review of case examples of sociologists in action who are acting as advocates for social justice and social change. They argue that citizen action can be promoted by increasing democratic participation in the production and implementation of knowledge and the creation of better human societies. If you become an advocate, you need to understand that you can use your research skills to create better human societies.

ENGAGING IN SOCIAL JUSTICE

In this section we introduce you to some definitions of **social justice.** We also address what might be expected of you as an advocate. After reading this material, some of you will find that you are far more comfortable with charity work than with advocacy. We hope you will see that it is important to be involved in changing social arrangements that benefit some groups and not others. Finally, two scholar activists in the Washington, D.C. area share with you their stories of how they pursue social justice. We include these in this guide so that you have examples of how faculty, students, and community members can work together.

DEFINING SOCIAL JUSTICE

David Jary and Julie Jary (1991) note that there are competing definitions of social justice. They suggest that some definitions of social justice emphasize the "assessment of the collective benefit" as being primary while other definitions emphasize "a balance of individual and collective rights" (1991, 256). Marullo and Edwards (2000, 899) state that social justice refers to "the state of institutional or structural arrangements in which there are no inequalities that are unjustifiable in terms of the greater social good or that are imposed unfairly." According to Mills (1959), the pursuit of social justice means informing the powerless of the structural causes of their social problems so that they can act to create social change.

Some sociologists note that social justice has been defined narrowly, including a primary focus on the distribution of resources (Feagin and Vera 2001; Young 1990). This narrow focus speaks to inequalities and how resources are distributed and how this distribution could be changed. Others take a broader perspective of social justice and injustices. Iris Young argues that social justice "means the elimination of institutionalized domination and oppression" (1990, 15). Injustices are the conditions that support oppression and domination of some groups by other groups in society.

Young identifies the importance of group differences and notes that it is important to attend to the idea that not all groups in society are equally situated in the social structure with regards to power and privilege. Social justice concerns the degree to which a society supports the social arrangements necessary for people to develop their capacities and express their experiences and to participate in determining their own actions without coercion (1990, 37).

Aspects of Social Justice

The type of sociology we are describing throughout this guide shares some similarities to what Feagin and Vera (2001) describe as liberation sociology. It is a sociology that has as its core the process of creating awareness of problems that exist in society that are structural and not the creation of individual characteristics. Practicing this type of sociology begins with several decisions: taking sides with the oppressed, listening, and empowerment (Feagin and Vera 2001).

Taking Sides with the Oppressed   Taking sides with the oppressed is counter to the traditional model of scientific research that argues that the researcher is in some way apart from those the researcher studies. Knowledge gained from bridging the university and the community in the pursuit of social justice is useful for empowering oppressed people in the community.

Listening   Taking the side of the oppressed requires listening to them. As you listen to people's stories and tales, you are learning about their culture, including values and themes (Rubin and Rubin 1995). You will learn in Chapter 2 that you use filters in how you listen. Are you really listening to their stories to learn how certain policies may affect their lives (McMillan 1998)? When you are engaged in dialogue with people who hold different cultural values from yours, you may feel uncomfortable or even angry. It may be hard to really hear their story, and thus to work with them to bring about change. With a commitment to taking sides with the oppressed, you must begin from their lived experiences. This requires you to be a critical listener.

Empowerment   The concept of empowerment, in the broad sense, refers to "participation of an agent in decision making through an effective voice and vote" (Young 1990, 251). Social justice means that all people in society should have the means to participate in decision making that affects their lives and choices.

Another way to look at empowerment is to define it in relation to its research methodology (Ristock and Pennell 1996). They draw from the work of Young (1990). They connect their definition to a societal level by viewing empowerment as a political activity that can range from individual acts of political resistance to mass political mobilization of relatively powerless groups.

Other aspects of social justice include three categories of nondistributive issues: "decision making procedures, the social division of labor, and culture" (Young 1990, 9, 22–23).

Decision-Making Procedures   Those who have the authority or freedom to make decisions also have the authority to set the rules and procedures that shape decision making.

Social Division of Labor   The social division of labor refers to how jobs or tasks are distributed among individuals and groups in society, as well as reflecting "an institutional structure [that] involves the range of tasks performed in a given position, the definition of the nature, meaning, and value of those tasks, and the relations of cooperation, conflict, and authority among positions" (1990, 23).

Culture   Culture refers to symbols, meanings, stories, and so on, through which people express themselves and through which people attach meanings to other people that "affect the social standing of persons and their opportunities" (1990, 23).

On the one hand, social justice includes decision-making procedures, social division of labor, and culture. On the other hand, social injustice involves the processes of oppression and domination. For some of you, these terms will be unfamiliar. For others, the use of language such as oppression and domination may make you feel uncomfortable. The use of particular language is often derived from the perspectives that sociologists use. We discuss this in depth in Chapter 3.

FROM A CHARITY TO A SOCIAL JUSTICE MODEL

There is considerable history to support the fact that acts of charity tend to end up reproducing the status quo (Marullo and Edwards 2000). There is also a history to support the fact that university and religious institutions have contributed to this

(Poverty Coalition UPdate 2002). Students who work in social service agencies in the community as part of their education are doing "for" the community rather than doing "with" them (Vogelgesang and Rhoads 2004; Ward and Wolf-Wendel 2000, 767). Doing for communities is implicit in a charity model where doing with emphasizes collaboration and mutuality. When the community collaborates, it owns part of the solution (Lewis 2004). It is no longer a passive recipient of what others want to give it (Ward and Wolf-Wendel 2000).

To illustrate: Some people believe that poverty is a natural form of social functioning. Others view poverty as an affliction and as a social problem calling for direct action. For centuries religious and secular organizations have addressed the problem, providing temporary relief to the poor as needed in the forms of food and clothing. Many of you have participated as volunteers in such charity programs. You have been exposed to the ideology of charity in your schools, churches, and other organizations. Today, some groups that are in need of funds to operate frequently approach people for contributions. In a charity model, an individual or group voluntarily shares resources of a variety of types with those who have fewer resources and are in need. When charitable work is run efficiently, with integrity, and gives to those really in need, it can save lives and maintain the dignity of recipients (Loeb 1999; Marullo and Edwards 2000, 899).

A basic premise underlying a social justice model is ". . . a social collective operates to maximize the well-being of all its members when all of its members have the abilities, resources, and opportunities to contribute to the greater good" (Marullo and Edwards 2000, 898). For Marullo and Edwards, the concept of social justice includes the themes of empowerment, integration, and transformation.

In a social justice model, you would be engaged in changing the structural and institutional practices that contribute to unjustified inequalities (Lewis 2004). There are laws that address social injustices people experience in our society because of race, sex, religion, nationality, ethnicity, sexual orientation, and disability status. However, many of these laws do not eliminate existing structural arrangements that reinforce these injustices. Thus, social inequalities continue. Social activists continue to work for civil rights even though civil rights laws were passed in the 1960s. Discrimination continues in this country. For example, according to The Sentencing Project (a national organization in Washington, D.C., that promotes reform in the criminal justice system), "African Americans account for 13 percent of the nation's drug users but 35 percent of drug arrests and 53 percent of drug convictions" (*Washington Post* 2003, A9).

In this guide we argue the need to move from a charity to a social justice model. While a charity model may ameliorate some of the unfortunate conditions for the poor in the short run, this model does not address the institutional arrangements in our society that perpetuate injustices in the long term. While more people may be volunteering to work on community projects today, this alone will not result in changes in the structural arrangements that contribute to social injustices.

If you have decided to participate in a service-learning advocacy program, expectations for you will likely differ somewhat from those in an internship program. Let us look at what might be expected of you.

BECOMING AN ADVOCATE

What might be expected of you if you want to be an advocate for social justice and make a difference in your own life and the lives of others? We expect that you will need to develop empathy and compassion for those groups experiencing inequalities, instead of judging these people on their individual characteristics. Practicing sociology means developing and using a *critical consciousness*. This consciousness opens the mind to see social problems as public issues, and as part of the social arrangements in society. Once aware of these public issues, a pursuit of social justice implies taking action to change these oppressive structures.

There are several aspects of becoming a student advocate for social justice. Some steps you might take include the following:

- Taking charge of your education
- Identifying and appropriating campus resources that are available to you
- Taking collective action to find the root causes of injustices (Mooney and Edwards 2001, 187)

As an advocate for social justice, you will want to participate in creating social change. You can advocate for many things, including changing norms and ideologies. For example, Martin Luther King, Jr. advocated for civil rights by participating in nonviolent demonstrations and delivering speeches. AIDS activists advocate for legal use of marijuana in treating AIDS patients by lobbying state and federal government officials, and pro-life groups advocate through public demonstrations and political lobbying for the elimination of the right of women to choose an abortion.

In order to create social change, some of the energy and time you give to volunteering must be spent on action directed toward the political roots of the crises we are experiencing. These actions are structural in nature and can be seen in public policy efforts to change government actions at all levels. Your participation in a well-designed service-learning advocacy program may well move you to a life-long commitment to social justice (Roschelle, Turpin, and Elias 2000). Such a commitment means you accept the idea that charity, while necessary and very helpful in some situations, is not a model to help solve social problems that are systemic in society. For example, food kitchens may be necessary in some situations, but to stop there does little to create institutional and social change.

You also need to be part of a larger public dialogue about the roots of social problems. You can continue to work as a volunteer in a soup kitchen that will always be necessary, even in the best of societies, but you need to find out why so many people continue to need assistance despite all the volunteer efforts to ameliorate such conditions. One way to address this is to talk about a concept of **witness** (Loeb 1999, 210).

> We can listen to those who come to the food banks, homeless shelters, and battered women's centers, and learn how they got there. We can talk to those on the street and hear their stories. We can work to understand why our society produces so much needless human pain. (Loeb 1999, 210)

However, you cannot stop after you hear the many stories. Applying the concept of witness means you must look for appropriate solutions.

One solution is "taking these examples and lessons to the village square—or its contemporary equivalent—and then doing our best to convey them to as many others as possible (Loeb 1999, 210)." One way for you to do this is to organize a protest against unjust conditions that can be changed with group action. For example, students at Georgetown University put pressure on the university administration to ban sweatshop labor from being used to produce campus products. This action gained support among students after a student visited a factory in Latin America and saw a cap with the Georgetown logo. The students organized a sit-in at the president's office after they became aware of all the issues that needed to be addressed by the university administration. As a further consequence of bringing about change in the university's practice, the students created a "code of conduct" that all vendors had to agree to follow. Over 200 campuses have accomplished similar successes (United Students Against Sweat Shops, http://www.usanet.org). In doing this, you help those who are oppressed become empowered to find their own voices and choices. You challenge the taken-for-granted myths that provide a cozy space for those who are empowered to ignore those who are not empowered. We share with you the stories of

Professors Walda Katz-Fishman and Sam Marullo who have challenged these myths as they work to create a cozy space to work with their students in the pursuit of social justice.

CONVERSATIONS WITH TWO SCHOLAR ACTIVISTS

We begin by having you read the life stories of two sociology professors who are currently working as scholar activists bridging the university and the community in Washington, D.C. The two stories are similar in many ways, and also quite different in how they practice sociology. They are both actively engaged with students, faculty, community members, and organizations. We include their stories in this guide because we believe their stories give you additional examples of how professors and students, working with community members, can pursue social justice.

Drawing from the thinking of Mills (1959), we asked Professor Walda Katz-Fishman and Professor Sam Marullo to share their life stories with us. We gave them three general topics to think about:

1. How has your history and biography shaped your commitment as a scholar activist?
2. What is it like to be a scholar activist in a university today?
3. What messages do you have for students on how to be social activists and to change social structure?

We did not tape record these conversations with Walda and Sam, but we gave them an opportunity to make any changes they saw as appropriate. We did not edit any of their stories.

Conversation with Professor Walda Katz-Fishman

We met with Professor Walda Katz-Fishman on a beautiful fall day in 2001, in her office at Howard University in Washington, D.C. Walda was very eager to share her time and stories with us about "the events that have made her what she is." Walda shared with us "what you need to know about me to understand my life as a scholar activist." We write this conversation in the first person, hoping that you can experience, in some ways, Walda's voice, her dedication, her passion, her vision, and her willingness to make her private life public in her pursuit of social justice and social change.

Getting Started in the South

I grew up in a liberal Jewish family in New Orleans, Louisiana. My parents were a part of the integration efforts and movement that started in the South. From slavery to the Civil Rights Movement, the South has seen and been part of oppression and liberation. There is a strong history of resistance and struggle there. I believe that my family was a strong influence on me becoming an organizer and an activist. One of my first "aha moments" was in the 1950s when I observed the domestic workers in our home who were of different class and ethnic background from my family.

Although I was alienated as an undergraduate student attending private school in New Orleans, I already had seen in some ways the effects of feminism in high school. I became "radicalized" in graduate school, attending Wayne State University in Detroit, Michigan from 1968 to 1970. Wayne State was a working-class school, and we shut the university down in response to the Vietnam War. It was there that I had my second "aha moment." Social theory was very important for helping me to understand the world. It was my reading of Karl Marx that provided me with an analysis and hook to the world—a framework combining alienation with humanism.

Moving On

While at graduate school, I became connected to the city. I had a mentor—Lynda Ann Ewen—who linked me to the League of Revolutionary Black Workers, a pro–working-class group, and other revolutionary groups. This was an era of militancy, humanism, and people's rights. In 1970, I moved to Washington, D.C., with my husband. I applied to many schools, and ultimately came to Howard University. Students at Howard University wanted to have African-American teachers, but I was hired because of my educational background, including Phi Beta Kappa, and the need for someone to teach such courses as social psychology and social theory. I am still excited about teaching social theory at the undergraduate and graduate levels.

Once in the academy, you have to "do a political analysis of your own situation." I had to strategize how I would survive the experience as a scholar activist. I knew that in order to make it in the academy and to survive you have to pay respect to where academics are. It is important to do ALL the professional things that academics do. I did that, and I have continued to do this by engaging in many faculty responsibilities, including being involved with organizations such as the American Sociological Association (ASA), the Society for the Study of Social Problems (SSSP), Association of Humanist Sociologists (AHS), District of Columbia Sociological Society (DCSS), and Sociologists for Women in Society (SWS). I also try not to bring the university, as an institution, into the model of strategy for activism. One just needs to create a space to share a progressive point of view. I never tried to make everyone embrace my position. You must learn about your organization and be good at managing internal politics within the university. But you don't try to take Marx to department meetings.

There are some students who are most receptive to activism and scholar activists need to build a student base. I have found this in teaching a course like social theory, where I can, as part of the course, present my perspective, which is historical materialism. For example, we study dialectical development where things are always in motion and move in contradiction. Capitalists think they will hold on to economic growth, but on the other hand you have 2 1/2 billion people living on $2 or less a day. Using this approach, some of my beliefs can be shared, couching them in social theory. I give the students a framework and encourage them to see where this ends up because we are in a crisis relative to poverty. On the other hand, I do not force students or the university to accept my agenda: One can never do that. I can take students into the community and share with them my ideas as long as I am doing this as a class, but not representing my ideas to be those of the department or university.

Scholar activists also need a community organization affiliation and base. We have to participate in political practice and in partnership in a community. In the late 1970s, I was involved in a Marxist study group where we explored what it would mean to have structural change. I continue to be linked to the community belonging to such organizations as the League of Revolutionaries for a New America. I believe that scholar activists have to reproduce ourselves; this can be done through mentoring, nurturing, and creating alternatives. My mentor in Detroit instilled in me the importance of being grounded in political organizations that are part of the community. This has been an important aspect of my activism. Community involvement begins with the university; you need a friend within the university to protect your back. When I arrived at Howard, I asked myself, "Who is a friend?" I found a friend in Ralph Gomes. He was very much into the profession and the university but grounded in working class organizations. There is the power of two, including a division of labor as well as protection.

Taking Social Action to the Street

Taking social action to the street means many things. First, there is the importance of political grounding. One needs to be bridged to an organization that is a social movement organization. This means, one needs to be part of an organization that has a presence, bringing working class people to the table as equals.

In 1986, I co-founded Project South with Jerome Scott in Atlanta, GA. It is now a 501(c)(3) non-profit organization. By 1986, I had tenure at Howard University. Project South has no formal relationship with Howard. We selected the name because of its historical context, in particular, coming out of the struggle to defend the electoral gains of the West Alabama Black Belt against the U.S. government's charges of alleged vote fraud in the South. Also, the South saw the beginnings of political attacks on women and workers' movements. People often think of the South as only a place of repression. They fail to see that there is lots of resistance by those oppressed. For example, abolition and civil rights began in the South. This resistance demonstrates the importance of ordinary people.

Project South brings an education focus: consciousness, vision, and strategy. Funding for the organization comes primarily from alternative funders such as the Funding Exchange (a network of community based funders), not mainstream foundations. We also do grassroots funding, including membership drives. In 1991, we formally incorporated as Project South: Institute for the Elimination of Poverty & Genocide, a community-based 501(c)(3). We asked ourselves what things we would eliminate to create justice and equality in the world? We decided to develop a systematic attack on genocide and poverty as a way of transforming society. Everyone has to understand that we all have vested interests in eliminating poverty. It affects all of us, for example, we have "gypsy scholars" in great numbers in the university as changes continue in education. As a community based organization, we sought to bring scholar and community activists together as equals to learn how to bring about social change on issues of poverty and genocide. The bridge between the university and Project South creates a safe space for taking social action to the streets. Popular education is a powerful way to bring about change.

My third "aha moment" came in 1995, with the importance of popular education. We need fun and creative ways to teach and learn. It is still a controversial idea to have working-class people speak for themselves. It is considered dangerous to let them do that. The Popular Education Initiative (PEI) has several programs, which include workshops for training people, book forums to encourage dialogue, and building community based organizations in the Southeast. We produce many materials together in partnership but these must be done in simple sentences that create a fun way to learn.

Working in this way is a safe space for students to start their engagement in a community. It is difficult, however, to bring students, scholars, and community members together. People in a community bring their experience to the table where each can learn from the other to build organizations that contribute to justice and equality. Then everyone can have an "aha moment" as they engage in another way to learn.

In response to your questions about how students can be involved in creating social change, I believe there are several ways. For example, teach students to reflect on how their lives are shaped by the same forces that create homelessness, poverty and so on. They should also think about how the same things will affect them in the future. They should think about their own lives and how systems impact on them. This includes middle-class white students, as well as other students. We are all affected by the negative effects of the system. It is not an us and them situation; rather the system comes down on all of us, just harder on some than on others. The system denies well-being to all or most of us. Today, our housing, health care, and education systems are failing all of us. Another example is we all need to understand why it is in our own best interests to eliminate a criminal justice system where young black men are increasingly being incarcerated. This will come back on all of us. We all need to reflect: coming back to our lived experiences, and thinking of what part we all can play in building today's movement for global justice and equality.

Conversation with Professor Sam Marullo

We met with Associate Professor Sam Marullo in late autumn, 2001, at his office at Georgetown University, Washington D.C. Sam was generous with his time and shared with us how he became a strong advocate of social action and service-learning. He has co-authored a book with Kerry Strand on community-based research and learning. He has written extensively with Bob Edwards, whom he mentored as a graduate student at Catholic University. We write this conversation in the first person, hoping that you can experience, in some ways, Sam's quiet voice, his contagious smile, and his passion for bridging the University and the community in the pursuit of social justice for the oppressed in society.

Growing Up as a White Male

I grew up in an upstate suburban working-class community in New York, a childhood highly unlikely to produce a scholar activist. The events that particularly transformed my life in terms of activism first occurred when I attended college. I started as a pre-med major and finished as a math major. I did my undergraduate work at Colgate University. Two sociologists had a large influence on me there: Professor Arnold Sio, from whom I took a Race Relations course, and Professor Warren Ramshaw, who inspired me to apply my newly acquired social research skills to address matters that were important to me.

During the 1970s, the university was just beginning to integrate. There were some sixty black students in a total student body of around three thousand students. It was my first real encounter with students who were not white like me. My first "aha moment" occurred in a sociology class on inequalities when we had to interview two people who were somehow "different" from ourselves. This became a transforming moment for me because the two black students that I interviewed took the time to educate me about civil rights. Some years later, at our tenth year reunion, I let them know of the significance this conversation had for me, but which for them was quite ordinary at the time. In this and other sociology classes, I became excited about applying scholarship to study inequalities.

These two sociology professors convinced me to go to graduate school to study sociology. During graduate school at Columbia, I became very involved in social movements, including civil rights, environmental, anti-nuclear, and women's movements. I had good faculty mentors who encouraged me to pursue my interests and develop a dissertation that would examine one of these areas in depth. My dissertation did focus on racial inequality, using mathematical modeling to examine housing discrimination against blacks.

Connecting to Social Movements

In the early 1980s, as I was completing my doctorate, I connected with the peace movement. At the time, I was teaching at Cleveland State University and I both worked with and studied the Nuclear Freeze Movement. A few years later, I moved to Washington D.C. to become actively involved in the national scene shaping policy to effect social change. I was interested in studying this process as well as trying to effect change, hoping to learn lessons about how grassroots organizations working for peace and justice could have an impact on national policy. I began teaching at Georgetown University, a Jesuit institution. The university is great in terms of supporting my work that focuses on social justice and for working with students who share these interests. In 1989, I spent one year as a fellow on Capitol Hill, which was an exciting time period when the Berlin Wall was falling. I used this opportunity to try to influence Congress by working from the "inside" to create legislation that would build new mechanisms for creating cooperation between East and West in place of the old "Cold War" divide. From this experience I wrote the book *Ending the Cold War at Home,* which led to my promotion and tenure as an associate professor, my current position.

I have been at Georgetown University for sixteen years. As a Catholic University, Georgetown is not as worried about the political repercussions of activism as some state supported universities may be. Georgetown is committed to be an engaged campus where students learn to be citizens and participants in a democracy so that they do not have to worry about the political consequences of taking the side of the oppressed. Our mission is to educate "men and women for others," which includes teaching students to be advocates on behalf of the disadvantaged. So we have students not only providing direct service, say to the homeless, but also students learning how to be advocates on behalf of the homeless and the poor. Throughout its history, the Catholic Church has taken the side of the oppressed. More recently, there has been a national move to force universities to be "engaged citizens" and devote university resources and teaching to solve community problems. Associations such as the Campus Compact and the American Association for Higher Education (AAHE) promote the concept of the engaged campus.

In general, Georgetown has been very supportive of my approach to service-learning, although there are professors who do not see activism as an educational process for students. Some purist faculty think students learn only in the lecture hall or in the library where they should be reading books. I believe that students learn best by applying their classroom- and book-learning to real life applications. This way, they learn not only the theory, but also develop the skills to apply their learning.

I have worn many hats since I've been at Georgetown. However, activism is where my heart and passion are even though applied sociology is often not valued by the profession in the form of promotion and other rewards. Early on I did participant observation in social movement organizations. It is not as easy now, as in the past, to do such research. Today, one has to explore social movements globally and look to how groups all share agendas. I see myself and colleagues as social movement scholars engaged today particularly in globalization movements. We are generating joint databases where we keep track of many features associated with the movements, including protest movements. We take students to observe the protest events and interview the participants. Both the service-learning course work and the social movements field work require that we prepare students ahead of time on how to behave and dress, so that they don't stick out at either a rally or in poorer neighborhoods. The university requires students to sign an informed consent statement that the risk management people and lawyers write and approve. This is all part of the educational mission of the university.

In the early 1990s, service-learning took me by storm. I attended a service-learning workshop at Stanford University in 1990. That was also a transforming moment for me. At this time, service-learning was creating its own language and models. By 1995, the "invisible college" was formed, and I was a part of this faculty association of people doing service-learning all around the country. Nearly ten years ago, I worked with a handful of colleagues at Georgetown to create the Justice and Peace Studies Program. It is an intellectual home for activist students and now nearly twenty-five students per year graduate from this program.

There are currently four courses on service-learning in the sociology/ anthropology department at Georgetown: Community Involvement Seminar; Women in Politics, where students work with a women's advocacy group; International Migration, in which students work with immigrant service or advocacy groups; and Project D.C. The latter course is my community based research course. Students do a collaborative research project with a community nonprofit organization. An exciting aspect of this course has been the addition of community people serving as co-instructors in the class. Students have the opportunity to hear the voice of someone who is living in oppressed conditions and working to change them. We often prescreen the sites to be selected by the students in this course. We create a directory with options of organizations that are generally non-profit and non-governmental organizations. For example, we do not have our students serve as interns on Capital Hill. Service-learning is not charity work here, but rather it is the university and community working together to undertake research that contributes to social change. And sociology adds a critical dimension to this work, providing students with a sociological imagination that enables us to see how society's structures and institutions underlie such inequalities and that it is social structures that need to be changed as the ultimate causes of injustice.

In the past year, I helped conceptualize what is now known as Georgetown's Center for Social Justice. I felt there was a real need to integrate the university's research and teaching with the community. An important part of this Center is the Community Research and Learning (CoRAL) network. Currently, we are developing a CoRAL Web site (http://www.coralnetwork.org) where community organizations can find faculty that can help them with their research needs. CoRAL is the umbrella organization and has a steering committee of faculty and community people who serve as decision makers for the group. We give small grants to help launch these collaborative projects.

At times, when I was on leave from Georgetown, I tried on different roles in the community. For example, I worked as a lobby activist to create change and also worked at the grassroots level as an organizer. However, I did not find these to be a good match with my personality. The University seemed to be the place where I felt most comfortable as a base for social change. Moreover, the university has many resources that may be more difficult to acquire elsewhere. These include grant money, lots of intellectual skills and resources, student labor, and the prestige of the University. The university has pockets of loose change for starting projects, for which we can then get grant funding. When we can get a million dollar endowment from the university for our Center, it is big money to undertake this kind of work. For these, and other reasons, it makes sense to me to use the structure within the University. In this way, the university can give back something to the community.

My Message to Students

In response to your question about what I say to students about social change, I stress the fact that any individual can participate in a social change movement. We discuss the experiences of people like Rosa Parks and Martin Luther King, Jr. They did not create the Civil Rights Movement by themselves. I tell them that there are many nameless, faceless people who disappear in history but have been involved in the everyday work of making social change. I don't ask students to change the world, but just to make small efforts toward changing it. I tell them not to set their expectations too high, but to take their tools and experience and use them. When their friends tell them they are too idealistic, I suggest they might want to find new friends who will support them and their dreams. We are all flawed people, but we can also make a difference by following our own passion. Each of us can find the way to be an activist. We can do activism within any job, using the skills we have learned. We need to think creatively, create safe spaces where we can nurture our ideals and commitments to justice, and learn how to put them into practice.

My passion is to create a movement within the university and of universities! Part of this passion includes recruiting and transforming students so that they become aware of how their actions have consequences. The most rewarding part of my teaching is when students say to me that they have learned through their community-based work how they can make a difference and that they want to continue on this path.

Now that you have read their stories, we hope that you have some sense of how Professors Walda Katz-Fishman and Sam Marullo work as scholar activists, and how they bridge the university and the community through practicing sociology. We also want you to reflect upon the nature of activism and the different strategies of activism that are possible in the pursuit of social justice. These two people share similarities in their commitments to make the educational experiences of their students more purposeful, and make this world a better place for all people to live. They differ, in part, in the strategies they use to carry out their commitment to practice sociology and to social justice.

ORGANIZATION OF THE GUIDE

Practicing Sociology in the Community, A Student's Guide is designed as a supplement to the text or readings provided for your course in community-based learning, such as service-learning advocacy, service-learning, or an internship program. It is organized to make it easier for you to connect what you learn in the classroom with your experiences in a community, and to take your community experiences back to the classroom, reflecting upon what these experiences mean for you and for the development of sociological knowledge. It is our purpose to illustrate ways of practicing sociology that are meaningful for advancing your sociological understanding as well as making a difference in a community and your personal life.

Practicing Sociology in the Community, A Student's Guide is divided into six chapters. Chapter 1 introduces you to the organization of this guide. Chapter 2 provides a description of what we mean by practicing sociology. As part of practicing sociology, you will learn to use a critical sociological approach and develop critical thinking. Chapter 3 identifies some of the cultural aspects of community that might be important for you to explore. It also provides some insights into discovering yourself and how your life might be shaped by your experiences in a community or organization.

In Chapter 4 you learn how to keep a journal and the importance of this effort in your community-based learning program. As part of the journal process, you will be engaging in critical reflection on the observations you make and the experiences you have in the community or organization. While doing this, you are examining your own personal beliefs and how these may shape your interpretations.

Chapter 5 focuses your attention on field research and how it is a means for bridging the university and the community. Many of you have had little opportunity to do field research and may find the steps involved to be challenging and perhaps somewhat overwhelming. We address some of the challenges you are likely to confront while practicing sociology in the community. In Chapter 6 we return to a more in-depth look at promoting social justice in the community and focus on the issue of poverty in the United States, and poverty among children in particular. We finish the guide by looking at how other students have become advocates for social justice with the hope that you will as well.

All chapters end with "Reflections." We include exercises for reflection to give you an added opportunity to learn about the processes of linking your course work with the community and taking what you have learned in a community back to your classroom. We also include exercises that may help you become an advocate for social justice.

CONCLUSION

We hope that practicing sociology is an important life-shaping event for you. We try to prepare you for the experience by raising issues and providing practical strategies throughout this guide that you may use in a community-based learning program. We encourage you to use a critical sociological approach and to develop critical thinking and reflection that will help you move beyond your own experiences.

REFLECTIONS

After reading this chapter you begin to understand why it is important for you to be curious about what is going on around you and how to use a critical sociological approach to make sense of what you have observed. You are aware now that you must use critical thinking and critical reflection to help you understand the structural arrangements of society; that understanding will move you beyond looking at individual characteristics to explain current social issues. We provide a few exercises for you to complete to help you in that process of looking beyond individual factors to explain social issues. We suggest that you keep these written exercises in the appendix of your journal and that you discuss your answers in class.

I. MEANINGS

Write in your own words the meanings of (1) critical thinking, (2) critical reflection, and (3) critical sociological approach. Illustrate each of these with examples from your observations and experiences.

II. PERSONAL INVENTORY

We ask you to do a self-inventory and put this in your journal. If you take this seriously, it will provide you with ideas on what kind of a community project would interest you, or where you might want to select your internship. We all have this information in our heads but putting these experiences on paper will give you data to use to reflect on your decisions. Writing is also good practice because it requires thinking and it helps to reduce confusion in our thinking. It should also reduce your frustration over how to get started.

1. What do you care about most? These can be personal activities, social issues, or a combination. List these in some priority of importance to you. Explain your reasoning for selecting these.
2. What do you care about least? For example, do you dislike writing, thinking, reflecting, the downturn in the economy, terrorism, poverty,

racism, and other social concerns? Again, list these in some order and explain your reasoning for each.

3. Do you have any hobbies or special skills that you would like to share with others? How did your interest develop in each of these—i.e., who was influential in shaping your interests? Your friends? Your parents?

4. List your skills that will be useful when doing a community-based learning program. For example, are you comfortable speaking in public; are you a good writer; are you a good organizer; and are you a good thinker? List in order and explain your reasoning for these choices.

III. CRITICAL REFLECTION

You pick up a newspaper and read the following from the *Los Angeles Times:* The most underrepresented group of Americans at the nation's top colleges and universities is not blacks or Hispanics, but students from low-income families. Only 3 percent of the freshmen at the 146 most selective colleges and universities come from families in the bottom quarter of Americans ranked by income. About 12 percent of the students on those campuses are black or Hispanic. There are four times as many African-American and Hispanic students as there are students from the lowest (income) quartile (Savage 2003).

Apply your understanding of critical thinking and a critical sociological approach to help you interpret these findings. You can see that there is less socioeconomic diversity in the colleges than racial or ethnic diversity. Can you explain these findings by individual factors? If not, reflect on what forces outside individual ones help you make sense of these. For example, is education structured in our system so that everyone is provided an equal chance of getting an adequate education to meet college entrance requirements? Do these findings surprise you? If yes, explain. If no, explain. Write a paragraph identifying what you see as the social issue in this report.

IV. COMMUNITY EXPERIENCES

We ask you to reflect on what you have read in this chapter by thinking and writing about your history to this point. You can begin by making a list, if you like, of your observations and experiences in the communities in which you have lived, including your educational communities. We ask you to do this as a first step in becoming engaged in what is happening around you so that you can begin to see where problems and issues may be present that need your attention. Remember, we are not asking you to change the world but you can make a small difference if you are engaged in what is happening around you. You can put your story in your journal so that you can reflect on it during the semester.

1. What did it mean to you to grow up in the community(ies) you lived in? Describe in detail the physical environment, major political environment, economic and social environments. For example, did you live in a safe community? Explain what being in a safe community means to you. Reflect on your writing by asking yourself to what extent you were engaged in shaping what happened within the community.

2. Describe what it was like to live with your family. There are many different types of families. What type of family did you live with? After describing your family, detail your place in this structure. How was authority distributed in your family? List the types of activities you did with your family, including any rituals such as those linked to religion and holidays. Now reflect on how these experiences might have shaped what you do and how you become engaged in community life.

3. Describe your educational experiences before you came to college. Now reflect on the opportunities you had to make choices about where you would go or what you would do in the future. Did you choose your college or did it choose you? Reflect on how these opportunities and decisions may influence your life chances of doing what you want to do.

4. Describe any experiences in which you were involved in community work as a volunteer or as an activist. Reflect on how you became involved; for example, did your class in school develop projects for community involvement? Did you belong to clubs that engaged in community issues? Reflect upon when your interest in becoming engaged in community work began. Can you think of one example where you may have made a small difference on a social issue?

V. CRITICAL THINKING

You were watching the television news and you heard the following information: Some colleges are using affirmative action practices to give equal chances to men to gain admission. Why? It seems that women make up 70 percent of college applications. According to the news, to make the college equally representative of men and women they suggest that they need to accept more men from the pool of applicants. Their explanation for the skewed application pool is that women are outperforming men at all levels of education. In fact, one analyst speculated that the last man to get a bachelors degree would be in 2068 unless affirmative action is used to keep the student balance of men and women.

What is on your mind when you read this? Apply your critical thinking to analyze these findings. What information would you need to have before you begin your analysis of these findings? Do you know what affirmative action means and how it is carried out? Do you have a view on whether affirmative action is a sound policy to reduce forms of social injustice? Do you have any thoughts as to why women are outperforming men in school? Does this match with your observations and experiences? Does the structure of our educational system support women's education over men's? Is this a war against boys, a title of an upcoming book?

CHAPTER 2

Practicing Sociology

Practicing sociology in the community is the focus of this guide. As an undergraduate student, you are about to embark on an important and informative journey that takes you outside your classroom and into the community. Exploring community life with a sociological lens is one way of looking at phenomena with a critical eye. Part of the excitement of this process is moving beyond your own personal experiences. You will learn how to evaluate evidence and arguments and you will begin to understand how you can make changes rather than just reacting to the world around you.

Generally, the broadest concept applied to practicing sociology in the community is "applied sociology." There are several definitions of this concept (Miller 1999). The American Sociological Association (ASA) suggests that applied sociology, which can range from clinical sociology to activism, starts with a problem in the community, and the application of sociological knowledge is used to create changes for the benefit of people in that community (1995). In this sense, the single most important objective is solving a specific problem. If the field of sociology is enriched by the experience, this is a bonus. From another point of view, applied sociology can refer to sociologists who make their names known in the community by writing editorials in newspapers or becoming expert witnesses in court trials (Miller 1999). You may want to read more about the meanings of applied sociology in sociological journals and on the Internet.

In this chapter, we explore the process of practicing sociology in the community. This includes what it means to practice sociology, the link between practicing sociology and structural relations, using a systematic approach to practicing sociology in a community-based program, and using critical thinking. Practicing sociology is only one way of thinking about the complexities of social life. Truth and understanding come to us in many ways, including faith, intuition, and authority, to name a few. We do not claim that practicing sociology is the only way to make sense of your community-based learning experience; it is our focus in this guide. The ability to practice sociology is the ability to analyze your experiences by focusing on the interconnections between individual social actions and relationships you observe, and the social forces that shape these interactions and relationships. Further, it is the ability to identify social problems, reflect upon these conditions, and take action, when possible, to end oppression and domination of some groups in society.

WHAT IT MEANS TO PRACTICE SOCIOLOGY

What does it mean to "**practice sociology**"? This is an important concept in this guide because practicing sociology is one means of linking your classroom experiences with the community. Practicing sociology comes from the idea of praxis that is

> purposive action, including political action, to alter the material and social world, including humanity itself. As a central general concept within Marxism, praxis draws attention to the socially constructed economic and social institutions and the possibility of changing these—people's capacity for freedom, which cannot be achieved entirely at the individual level. (Jary and Jary 1991, 381–382)

Praxis is a complex activity. Step one begins with action. As you practice sociology in a community, you must first understand "what makes a problem problematic" (Bean 1996, 3). Historically, there have been so many phenomena identified as social problems that it may be difficult for you to comprehend how it is possible to identify social problems. There is no set procedure for doing so and no particular people or group that is appointed to define social problems (Baker, Anderson, and Dorn 1993). However, we do have some suggestions. Practicing sociology means starting with the premise that all social problems are **socially constructed**. That is, they are created and sustained by some groups in society. Over time, these patterns of relationships become part of the social structure and shape the lives of people in various ways. In other words, you must take into account the social context in which phenomena are situated.

What is important as you begin to explore social conditions is to be curious about the world around you. To do this you must be engaged. Identifying social problems is a "mental habit" you develop. Why are things the way they are? Why do some people seem to have so much while others struggle just to survive? To be engaged and wonder about the society and the world you live in is a learning process. You may find it difficult to identify problems but you can learn how to determine the nature of social problems as you practice sociology. The two most important points are challenging your own assumptions and opening your mind to many points of view. We elaborate on these points throughout this guide.

Step two of praxis involves reflection. As we mentioned in Chapter 1, reflection is a process of examining experiences in the community or an organization and applying your classroom knowledge to gain a new understanding of social conditions. This is your opportunity to link community-based learning activities with classroom experiences. It should also prepare you for step three by highlighting your awareness of community needs.

Step three of praxis is a return to action in the form of advocacy, aimed at changing oppressive and dominant structures. Sociologist Todd Gitlin describes activists as people whose "beliefs hook up with their activities." He goes on to say that "an activist refuses to take the world for granted" (2003, 4). If you decide to be an activist, you are going against the norms of an organization, community, or society. If you are participating in a service-learning advocacy program with a focus on people who are homeless, you might be involved with housing issues, trying to help the community change existing laws that discriminate against some groups and may result in people becoming homeless. Some of you might become advocates for homeless people trying to find alternatives to the current economic problems or medical problems that many of these people face each day. Not all of you will be advocates for change, challenging the status quo. However, we hope that many of you will decide to make improvements in people's lives when you are faced with injustices, not only in your community-based learning program but throughout your lives.

Practicing sociology is a particular way of thinking and doing that allows you to understand how individuals and groups are active participants in shaping their social world. However, these actions are constrained and enhanced by the social structures in which individuals and groups participate. You are an active participant when you begin to ask questions regarding what you observe, including questioning your own assumptions. You might observe women who are homeless carrying out some of their daily tasks in public restrooms and think they are too lazy to work. You may know people at your university who use drugs and believe they are too weak to say no to drug use. Or you may notice that women in your place of worship have fewer leadership roles than men and may believe these women are not interested in being leaders or have accepted doctrines that prohibit them from becoming involved in positions of leadership. All of these are stereotypes that serve to exclude certain groups. Social life is so complex that you must be willing to question your own assumptions and set them aside if you find them to be incorrect.

Practicing sociology is also a means for uncovering the **interconnections** of people's lives, a complex process in which you evaluate events that are greater than the people you observe. You can't understand homelessness by only observing these women in public restrooms. You must also explore the social arrangements and historical context that shape their lives. For example, you need to consider how laws that kept them from fully participating in the political and economic systems have marginalized women. Until the twentieth century, U.S. law prohibited a wife from owning property or signing contracts in her own right. Women could not vote in the United States until the passage of the Nineteenth Amendment to the Constitution in 1920. Susan B. Anthony worked her entire adult life for woman's right to vote. She died at the age of eighty-six, fourteen years before suffrage was ratified (Loeb 1999). Look at how gender relations are structured and how they may contribute to oppression. This type of critical inquiry leads you into the process of looking at structural arrangements.

We use the concept of practicing sociology because it draws attention to the concepts of **learning** and **process**. In certain types of community-based programs, you are *learning* sociology and applying it through a *process* that focuses on **structural explanations**, **systematic examination**, and **critical thinking** (Eckstein, Schoenike, and Delaney 1995). The notion of *process* is a key element because it takes time to learn and apply sociology; it is a process of trial and error. Let us look at how you can learn about structural relations and how the understanding of these relations will help you practice sociology in a community-based learning program.

PRACTICING SOCIOLOGY AND STRUCTURAL RELATIONS

Exploring structural relations in society means that you must acknowledge the limitations of thinking in terms of individuals when practicing sociology. Allan Johnson (1997) uses the metaphor of the forest and the trees to describe the process of moving beyond individual explanations for social phenomena. Mills (1959) calls this process the **sociological imagination**. According to Mills, the sociological imagination is our ability to see how social conditions affect our lives. The sociological imagination embodies the idea of praxis. It helps us to connect our individual experiences (what Mills calls personal troubles) with the historical period and institutional arrangements (society) in which we live. The following quote highlights the importance of using the sociological imagination when participating in community-based learning programs.

> Many undergraduates today demonstrate impressive levels of civic engagement in the form of community service. They serve meals in soup kitchens, work in homeless shelters, and staff AIDS hot lines. They work as interns in a variety of social agencies. Too few of them, however, are able to raise their eyes to the level of policy and social structure. They need the sociological imagination to see how their on-the-ground activities fit into a bigger picture, so that more of them can cross the bridge from serious moral commitment to effective political participation. (Shapiro 2000, A1)

Practicing sociology allows you to explore social life as it occurs in communities, organizations, and other field sites as you analyze the ever-changing connections of people and the social structures in which they participate. The organization of these patterns constrains choices, thinking, and feelings. To illustrate: If you are participating in a service-learning program in a not-for-profit organization, it has an existing social structure that patterns the behavior of the people in the organization. This is so because organizations usually have a mission, set goals and objectives, and form policies that create structure. As a participant, you will probably be exposed to a power structure in which some people get things done to meet their goals while others are powerless to force their wishes on the organization. Without structure, it would be extremely difficult to participate in social life.

How are *you* linked to the social structure? **Status** is the social position that you occupy in society. Along with that status come rights, entitlements, and powers. You confront social structures, for example, at school, in many different types of community-based learning programs, and within your families, based on your status. You participate in the status of student at the university and the status of an advocate in a service-learning program. Status is relational, for example, you cannot describe your status as student without referring to "teacher."

If you are participating in a community-based learning program with a focus on criminal justice, you are likely to see a hierarchy of statuses in the criminal justice system, ranging from those in power who make the laws governing which acts and processes are considered criminal, to those people in prison who are labeled criminals. Elijah Anderson (1990) wrote a book entitled *Streetwise: Race, Class, and Change in an Urban Community*, based on a case study he worked on for fourteen years. Those of you involved in a community-based learning program related to criminology will be especially interested in this study.

In social work settings, you are likely to confront the status of women and children in this society. Ruth Sidel (1996) wrote *Keeping Women and Children Last*, a book addressing the political economy of the United States and how poverty affects women and children more than it does men. Sidel argues that politicians divert attention away from the issues of poverty. More recently, Roslyn Arlin Mickelson edited a book entitled *Children on the Streets of the Americas* (2000) in which various case studies help illustrate the status of children living on the streets, and how political and economic relations have created even greater problems for these children.

Sociologists assume that understanding society requires more than understanding the motivation and behavior of individuals. Most of you who read this guide have grown up in a society rooted in individualistic thinking and behaving. Thus, it may be difficult to grasp the idea that understanding social life, including your experiences in a community, involves more than the personalities and behavior of the people you will interact with for the duration of your program. Sociologists look at **social groups**, "a collective of persons differentiated from at least one other group by cultural forms, practice, or way of life" (Young 1990, 43). The social groups to which you belong, which exist only in relation to other groups, shape your identity. Through social processes, social groups exhibit division of labors, for example between men and women, and young and old, to name a few. Practicing sociology means looking to structural explanations for understanding the injustices some groups experience in everyday life. Injustices are a part of the structure of society, often reinforced by people of privilege. Understanding that various groups in society live with oppression and domination because injustices are systemic in society, not because they are unwilling to do something about it, is an important aspect of practicing sociology.

Mills (1959) provided his readers with some basic guidelines for practicing sociology. In particular, his discussion of personal troubles and public issues focused on structural explanations for human behavior. He distinguished between personal troubles and public issues.

> Each of us can understand our own experiences and our own sense of meaning only by first locating ourselves within society and then by becoming aware of other individuals in the same societal and/or historical circumstance. What is essential here is the realization that knowledge about "self" depends upon knowledge about others and about *external societal realities* [italics in text]. (Goodwin 1997, 26)

Mills spoke to the difficulty of people gaining awareness of social conditions influencing personal lives. He states that students of sociology, through research, can identify the structural issues regarding social relationships and can use this information to inform those who are most affected and have limited power to create change. This is likely to be as true today as in the past.

Examples of personal troubles that are public issues include diseases. Diseases are generally the result of social rather than individual problems. The causes of cancer are varied but some forms of cancer can be attributed to living in areas where there is contamination of one form or another. Toxic waste is more likely to be found near areas where the poor live or work. Anorexia is more than just one's choice not to eat. It is linked to a society that glorifies thinness through its advertising, movies, and clothing designs. Whether or not to take illegal drugs is more than just saying no, an individual response. Illegal drug use is linked with an economic system that has unemployment structured into its design and a political system that makes the use of some drugs against the law. Mills compels us to look at personal troubles as public issues. That is, to look at how social forces create problems that are born out of social interaction, not personal characteristics.

PRACTICING SOCIOLOGY USING A SYSTEMATIC APPROACH

We assume that practicing sociology in the community is most valuable when you come prepared with a systematic approach that transcends your immediate observations. In this section, we explore some of the components of a systematic approach. We include thoughts about the paradigms and concepts that will guide your experiences in a community. The paradigms and theories you apply shape the questions you ask and the design of your research. Underpinning these is a knowledge of the social problem you are interested in pursuing. If you decide to do an internship your topic will generally come from course material and library research. If you are participating in service-learning advocacy, the questions are likely to come from the community.

Sociologically it is important to move beyond your own personal experiences. Paradigms help you to explore social life, which consists of the activities and behaviors that people engage in to build their social world, by providing you with a framework to move beyond your own experiences. Social life is too complex and its phenomena too diverse to be explained by a single point of view. Here are five aspects of a systematic approach to understanding the social world: "multiple forces shaping the social world," "social life occurs on different levels," "social life is relational," "people make choices reacting to their social world," and "measurement error" (Pettigrew 1996, 11–15). Following each aspect, we discuss how it may be important to you when practicing sociology in a community-based learning program.

Multiple Forces Shaping the Social World

Because one factor is unlikely to cause an event, sociologists most often look at multiple forces that shape social life. For example, the relationships of social class and race shape social mobility. If you are trying to understand gender relations in an organization, you must look to such social relations as economic, class, ethnic, and race that intersect with gender relations (Hearn 1998) to help make sense of your observations.

Social Life Occurs on Different Levels

As suggested earlier in this chapter, sociological analysis does not stay at the level of the individual. Given the complexity of social life, you must look at broader structures in society, for example the political system, medical system, legal system, and economic system. At the highest level, sociologists look at entire societies. At the level of face-to-face interactions, they look at statuses, roles, norms, symbols, and so on.

Social Life Is Relational

Social life consists of many parts, linked in complex ways that we call patterns. For example, if a homeless shelter is your field site, you will find that there are relational links between the expectations of the people who come to the shelter to stay and the routines of eating, showering, and sleeping imposed by shelter personnel. These links, among others, make up the social structure within the shelter.

People Make Choices Reacting to Their Social World

Unlike the physical sciences where the major variables chosen for analysis are inert, people react to each other. They impose their own meanings on events. When you are in the community, exploring the various meanings that people attribute to objects, events, concepts, and processes is very important.

Measurement Error

When studying various phenomena, we sometimes assign numbers in order to study these events systematically. For example, you may take an I.Q. test and receive a score of 130. Unless you understand the basis for this number, it is meaningless. If you know that 100 is the average I.Q. score, you have one data point by which to begin to evaluate your own. However, any problem or distortion in how your score reflects what it is supposed to measure (intelligence) is known as measurement error. Sociologists looking at I.Q. tests have identified problems with these tests, including cultural biases. You may also be a source of measurement error as you practice sociology in a community or organization. How is this so? Your own biases and assumptions, based on your personal experiences, can distort your interpretations and analysis. At the same time, practicing sociology means accommodating the fact that you are a part of the society you are studying. Applying critical thinking is one method for considering all possibilities and not being blinded by your own assumptions and experiences.

To account for the complexities of social life, sociologists study social phenomena from various levels. For our purposes, we discuss the micro-level of social relations and the macro-level of social structures. These levels are not found in life. Rather, sociologists impose these levels of analysis on situations as a device for studying social life by breaking down its complexities. You must always be mindful of how these levels of analysis relate to each other as well as the fact that they overlap.

MICRO-LEVEL OF SOCIAL RELATIONS

Micro-level of social relations refers to social relations that involve face-to-face interactions such as those found in families, among workers, and friends. **Language**, which refers to a collection of symbols and rules for their usage, is one of the tools to construct micro-level interactions. It is language that allows us to give meaning to objects or events. Perhaps you have noticed that if you do not have a name for something, you are unlikely to notice it. This is an issue that is important to remember. You may be at a field site where many things are new to you. It is imperative to learn the language of your organization. One way for you to do this is to ask for meanings of new words you hear, and keep a list of these in your journal (see Chapter 4).

The micro-level consists of the following and we encourage you to think of more:

1. Attitudes refer to positive or negative evaluations of people, objects, or situations that predispose you to feel and behave negatively or positively toward them.
2. Beliefs refer to statements about what we term to be real.
3. Self refers to feelings and beliefs about ourselves.
4. Symbols are characteristics of objects, words, or gestures that mean more than themselves.
5. Social interactions refer to a process by which people act in relation to one another.
6. Social construction of reality refers to the process that people use to create or construct reality.

If you focus on the face-to-face interaction among women in a homeless shelter, you can learn how language shapes the meaning of homelessness for these women. In his book entitled *Tell Them Who I Am: The Lives of Homeless Women* (1993), Elliot Liebow records some of the language used by these women to describe homelessness. For some, the situation they found themselves in was not homelessness but rather "familyless" (1993, 81). For some of these women this meant the very difficult experience of being separated from relationships with their children. For other women, the homeless women in the shelter were their families. Exploring language is focusing on the subjective aspects of social life and, thus, the micro-level of social relations. Spoken and written language is a crucial aspect of social relations and creating structures.

MACRO-LEVEL OF SOCIAL STRUCTURES

Macro-level of social structures refers to large-scale structures and social processes, for example, the economy, government, institutions, and other cultural forces that shape people's lives. The macro-level seems external to us as individuals for we are born into a society that already has structure. That is, the macro-level already exists prior to us. Moreover, because of its existence it is coercive and shapes our behaviors and actions by making some choices seem far more apparent than others. To illustrate: Work in this society tends to be structured in a particular way. It is generally competitive, hierarchical, and profit-oriented. Thus, competing with others in your classroom or at work is not likely to seem unusual to you. To do otherwise might make you feel uncomfortable or make you seem lazy or a daydreamer during school. Nor should the idea that companies are in business to generate profits and keep stockholders happy be an unfamiliar role for business. Companies are not in the business of creating jobs. As individual workers, our lives are shaped by these structures. Many people face unemployment when companies close down because of economic troubles or move their businesses to countries outside of the United States.

The macro-level consists of the following and we encourage you to think of more:

1. Institution refers to patterns of social interaction with relatively stable structures that persist over time. Institutions have structural properties: (a) They are organized, and (b) they are shaped by cultural values. Although there is not full agreement about the number of institutions, generally family, economy, politics, education, health care, government, and media are identified.

2. Society refers to interacting people in a relatively defined territory who share a distinctive culture and distinctive institutions, although some sociologists question the relevance of this definition in a "globalizing world." (Jary 1997)

3. Social system refers to interrelated arrangements of institutions, in which social action is sometimes seen as performing social functions. Although some early sociologists viewed systems as being like biological systems, today sociologists recognize systems as variable and not maintaining the level of integration likely in biological systems.

4. Organization refers to two or more social systems related to each other through shared goals and expectations.

5. Nation refers to people who have a common symbolic identity that is based on a shared culture, as reflected in the same history, language, ethnicity, and/or religion.

6. Culture refers to the shared knowledge, beliefs, and values of members of a particular group. It is conveyed by one generation to another through the process of socialization.

Sociologists are interested in the interplay between micro- and macro-levels of society. Links between these various aspects of social life create social structure and are a primary focus of sociologists. It is likely that you will need to integrate both micro- and macro-levels of analysis. Not only will this help you understand social life, but it will also make it easier for you to participate in your community-based learning program and gain skills for future employment.

Because social life is complex, you will need some kind of framework as a guide to make your experiences and observations in a community or organization manageable. We begin by describing four paradigms commonly used in sociology. We also look at creating and using a conceptual framework. Selecting a paradigm and creating and using a conceptual framework will help you take a more systematic approach to practicing sociology.

PARADIGMS

Paradigms are broad perspectives that you can use for thinking about and organizing your understanding of social phenomena and their complexities. Paradigms are sometimes referred to as world views. Controversies arise in sociology, in part, because of the various paradigms that are used, all of which have different underlying assumptions about the world we live in and whose assumptions are not tested in research.

We present a brief discussion of four paradigms: functionalism, conflict, symbolic interactionism, and feminism. Remember that our discussion is very general. Within each paradigm you will find much variety. For example, the feminist paradigm contains many different forms of feminism, including liberal feminism, marxist feminism, socialist feminism, and radical feminism, often with conflicting assumptions.

Functionalist Paradigm

Functionalism assumes that society is an adaptive social structure that functions in ways to contribute to the maintenance of social systems. One assumption is that all systems in society are interrelated, making the analogy that society is like a living organism. Functionalists reason that a healthy society is one that is based on consensus and stability, thus de-emphasizing change and focusing on the status quo or equilibrium. In other words, the focus is on social order.

If a system is not functioning properly, it disturbs social stability and must be fixed. As might be expected, it is not always easy to determine if a system is not working properly. This is often a political question. To illustrate: According to an article in the *Washington Post* (Goldstein 2003), medical students, interns, and residents learn how to perform medical procedures by practicing on patients in teaching hospitals. One such procedure is a pelvic exam. At George Washington University Hospital, during April 2003, a patient going into the hospital for removal of an ovarian cyst asked her physician if medical students would be practicing pelvic exams on her while she was unconscious for the removal of the cyst. Her physician said yes. According to the article, this practice goes on in many teaching hospitals throughout the United States. Moreover, women are not routinely advised about this training and are not given the choice to refuse to allow medical students, interns, and residents to practice pelvic exams on them while they are unconscious.

What is your reaction to this story in the *Washington Post*? How would you go about verifying the information you have just read? For example, would you interview medical students, get information from the American Medical Association, or call the American College of Obstetricians and Gynecologists? Do you believe that performing procedures on unconscious patients (not related to their medical condition) is a legitimate way to train medical students, interns, and residents? Are there alternative ways of training them? Write down your answers to these questions. Try to open up your mind to the many points of view regarding this issue.

Sociologists who reason as functionalists argue that the social structures that meet the social needs of societies are called **institutions**. Each institution meets some of the needs or goals of society. These functions, easily observed consequences that create adaptation, are called **manifest functions**. For example, education functions to teach people to read. Unintended and often hidden consequences produced by institutions are called **latent functions**. For example, education has the latent function of teaching students values such as obedience to authority, respect, and efficiency that are useful for creating the work force of the future. Further, these messages for students vary, based on their race, class, and gender. To illustrate: In general, upper-class white males are more likely to receive messages to go to college and be prepared for careers in upper management while Hispanic and African-American males from lower-class families are more likely to be pushed toward vocational skills.

The functionalist paradigm focuses on various institutions in society (health, work, family, government, school, and so on) and the achievement of a stable society when these institutions work together. When using this paradigm, you assume that social arrangements are based on consensus. A functionalist might ask, "What are the functions of various institutions in society and how do they help to maintain stability?"

Conflict Paradigm

The **conflict paradigm** focuses on the social organization and conflict that are built into social relations and reasons that conflict and change are central to social organization and social life. While sociologists who use the conflict paradigm may speak of systems, they usually do not do so in the manner of functionalists. Rather, using the conflict paradigm means viewing systems as producers of conflict and inequality. In general, those who use the conflict paradigm view social conflict as paramount to structuring social life. More particularly, Karl Marx viewed class conflict as paramount because he argued that capitalism ultimately divided people into two classes, with the capitalists exploiting the workers, thus generating conflict.

The conflict paradigm assumes that society is structured so that some groups enjoy privileges and resources that give them the ability to exercise power and influence the implementation of strategies for change. A conflict paradigm views the distribution of **power,** the ability to control the actions of others regardless of their wishes, as fundamental to exploring social life.

Those who use the conflict paradigm assume that society is held together even though conflict is ubiquitous. For example, some sociologists accept that social order is maintained by political oppression, extension of welfare benefits, and spreading value consensus by the mass media, although conflict will never be resolved (Bradley 1997). A conflict theorist might ask, "Which groups gain from current social arrangements and which ones lose?"

Symbolic Interactionism Paradigm

Symbolic interactionism focuses on face-to-face interactions and argues that people and society are the result of social interactions based on language and other symbols such as gestures or objects. Interaction refers to actors taking into account others when they act (Charon 2001). Unlike those who use functionalism or conflict paradigms, those who apply symbolic interactionism paradigm view interactions rather than relationships as primary. What humans say and do, according to this paradigm, is a consequence of how they interpret the world they live in.

Symbolic interactionism assumes that people have the power to define society through their ability to create their own sets of meanings. The world is continually changing, according to symbolic interactionists, because meanings change over time. For example, money means nothing by itself; it does not have an objective meaning beyond green paper. It exists as a means of exchange only because of the social meaning attributed to it and the consequences of that meaning for patterning social action (Reiman 1996). Sociologists refer to this as the social construction of reality, meaning the process that people use in society to create or construct reality. We see our social world and make sense of it through interpretation, learning "through certain frameworks we have learned or shared" (Charon 2001, 119). Sociologists using the symbolic interactionist paradigm examine this process.

In general, symbolic interactionism assumes individual interactions and interpretations are the most fundamental in understanding and explaining social life. Symbolic interactionists might ask: "What meanings do people attribute to objects or events?" "How does language shape social interactions?"

Feminist Paradigm

In general, the **feminist paradigm** contends that the dominance of men over women is of fundamental importance to understanding and explaining social life. For example, they would focus on how masculine values, beliefs, and shaping of language place women in the untenable position of defining themselves from the point of view of men. Thus, gender is a core concept in how social life is organized. Feminism assumes that the organization of society and culture have been dominated by men to the exclusion of women. For example, some feminists suggest that in marriage women labor to benefit men but without "comparable remuneration." Similarly, in agricultural societies, women produce the products that men take to market, but usually men receive the status and income from this labor (Young 1990). As such, women have been marginalized. That is, they are outside the mainstream system of labor and labor does not or will not use them in most societies. In Western societies this is seen in terms of single mothers as well as many other groups, including young black males, people with disabilities, and the elderly. The feminist paradigm, in its great variety, views the importance of women gaining control over their own lives.

Feminist research today focuses on the oppression of women and their empowerment. It does this in a way that differs from many other paradigms in sociology. For example, it tends to begin with the everyday lives of women. Dorothy Smith wrote in *The Everyday World as Problematic* (1987) that starting from the "standpoint of women," meaning the view from women's experiences and situations, is the way to free women from the male-dominated discipline of sociology where the models and assumptions do not fit with the organization of life as women experience it.

You are likely to read in many books that there are several varieties of feminist thought, including liberal feminism, marxist feminism, socialist feminism, postmodernist feminism, radical feminism, multicultural feminism, and so on. Here are some issues and questions that might be asked from a feminist paradigm. Feagin and Vera (2001, 214) provide one example that has been influenced by feminist theory. "The issues dealt . . . with how categories such as 'gay,' 'lesbian,' and 'straight' are social and culturally constructed and how these categories serve to define positive and negative identities and to include and exclude people within communities." Some feminists might ask questions regarding women's access to ways in which resources are distributed in society. Others might ask questions regarding the economic structures in society and how they oppress women, while other feminists might focus on the patriarchical systems that oppress women, particularly through violence.

Sociologists tend to frame their research within the context of paradigms. During your community-based learning program, use these paradigms to help formulate your questions. You should consider which paradigms are more likely to lend themselves to social change, advocacy, and the pursuit of social justice. Next we explore how conceptual frameworks will help guide your experiences in a community or organization.

CREATING AND USING A CONCEPTUAL FRAMEWORK

In general, a **conceptual framework** "is a formulation of what you think is *going on* with the phenomena you are studying—a tentative *theory* of what is happening and why" (Maxwell 1996, 25). Joseph Maxwell says that a conceptual framework or context includes "the system of concepts, assumptions, expectations, beliefs, and theories that supports and informs your research" (1996, 25). It is important to note that you build your conceptual framework, but you do so with the help of theories that others have already developed. However, as Maxwell states, sometimes these theories are flawed and, therefore, you must critically examine them. Later on in this chapter we discuss critical thinking in more detail.

Your conceptual framework is also informed by your working in a community: This is your experiential knowledge. Maxwell provides seven questions that can help you reflect on your experiential knowledge. He suggests writing memos to document these experiences. Your journal would be a good place to record them (see Chapter 4).

1. The thing I am most excited about in my study is. . . .
2. My main hope for this study is. . . .
3. The main thing I am afraid of in doing this study is. . . .
4. The biggest assumption I am making in my research is. . . .
5. The main way that this research draws on my own experience is. . . .

6. One thing I'm sure of about what's going on is . . . .
7. I would be really surprised if, as a result of the research, I learned. . . . .
   (Maxwell 1996, 56–57)

Exploring existing theory and developing theory are part of practicing sociology and creating a conceptual framework. It is fun! When you consider an idea and apply a concept that helps you make sense out of some aspect of your social world, it is exciting; you have opened a new window to help you view life.

The process of theorizing can begin in several different ways. For example, you can begin with theory to help you understand the relationships between individuals and the broader social context or you can develop a theory to increase your understanding of these relationships. Terry Williams in *The Cocaine Kids* (1989) analyzes the lives of young people in New York who deal drugs, by being a participant observer in their culture. He relies largely on these young people to tell their stories about drug dealing and drug use. William Foote Whyte's book *Street Corner Society: The Social Structure of an Italian Slum* (1943) is a classic case study of community life. His analysis came from the observations and communications he had with people in "Cornerville." Other researchers begin, not with the people they are studying, but by theorizing about structures that constrain or enable their relationships. In practice, linking sociological theories and community-based research is neither applying theory nor developing it. Research is often a process of moving back and forth between the two. However, as Bruce Berg (2001, 16) notes: "Every research project has to start somewhere. Typically, this starting point is an idea."

Theory

A **theory** is a set of interrelated statements used to explain a phenomenon. People often think of theories as something used only in scientific endeavors. This is incorrect for we all use theories every day to help explain events. We all have ideas about how things work. For example, ask your parents why people are on welfare in this country. Ask your peers about drug use on campus or teenage pregnancy. Most will have theories to explain these events. Moreover, if you ask your peers how a community-based learning program works at your university, some will have ideas. However, scientific theories differ from other theories, in part because scientists look for evidence to refute their theories. In your daily life, you may be satisfied if your own experiences support your theories.

Some sociologists arrive at explanations and understandings by applying theories. For example, Jay MacLeod used social reproduction theory to help understand the lives of two groups of working class teenagers, one white and one black, who live in public housing in his book entitled *Ain't No Makin' It* (1995). Social reproduction theory is a structural approach that tends to help us understand the structures that enabled and constrained these young men. As you read the book, however, you will quickly see that the young men MacLeod interviewed did not generally describe their experiences in terms of economic systems or race. Rather, they spoke to their own ambitions and their difficulties in school and getting jobs. MacLeod interpreted their experiences guided by theory. This theory may be useful for you if you have access to social services organizations or the criminal justice system during your community-based learning program.

You may find that relating sociological theory to events in the field is difficult. It takes practice to "do" sociology. Carefully chosen community-based learning program sites can help to bring together the tools of sociology you learn in the classroom with life experiences. Charles Green (1999, 7) argues that abstraction and experiential learning (community-based learning programs) are not opposites but rather "complementary phases" of the application of theoretical knowledge to everyday experiences.

Not only can you apply theories, but you can also develop your own theory. There are several texts and articles written on this subject; one of the most widely known is *Grounded Theory* by Anselm Strauss and Judith Corbin, editors (1997). However, for your purpose of practicing sociology, a less formal approach is likely and probably more useful for you. For example, you can begin by linking two concepts together. Maxwell (1996) calls this a "barbell theory." What you want to do is propose a relationship between the two concepts. For example, "patriarchy leads to violence by men against women." As your community-based learning program progresses, you are likely to develop more sophisticated theories.

In sum, Leonard Beeghley provides us with a thought-provoking notion about doing theory. He suggests that we do the following:

> Imagine putting a jigsaw puzzle together without using the edge pieces. To make the task even harder, imagine doing it without looking at either the box cover or the pictures on each individual piece. These bits of information are important because they provide a useful frame of reference for understanding the puzzle. As such, they guide us in putting it together by helping us to see relationships among the pieces that might otherwise go unnoticed. Without such orienting cues, assembling the puzzle becomes much more difficult, perhaps impossible. I would like to suggest that the edge pieces, box cover, and pictures on the pieces are analogous to a theory in that they provide a way of making sense out of what would otherwise seem chaotic. (1997, 267)

The paradigm from which you view your social world also shapes this puzzle solving. Community-based learning programs are a practical and effective way to begin transition from theory to application, from classroom to the community, in the pursuit of social justice.

Concepts

Thus far in this section, we have briefly discussed paradigms and the general ideas of a conceptual framework. Now we turn to the use of concepts. They are one of the most important elements of practicing sociology with a systematic approach.

Concepts are the basic language of sociology and its theories; they are the "building blocks of theory" (Pettigrew 1996, 34). *Concepts are abstractions and the tools used to communicate ideas and make sense of the social world.* Identifying and using them attaches meaning to objects or events. People cannot learn about abstractions apart from experiences (Green 1999). Community-based learning programs provide you with the experience to apply concepts to help analyze events, objects, and relationships in the community.

Sociological concepts extend "everyday language" and commonsense understanding of social reality (Jary 1997). To illustrate: Here are some selected commonsense statements that many people in the United States hold true.

1. Poor people are far more likely than rich people to break the law.
2. The United States is a middle-class society where most people are more or less equal.
3. Most poor people don't want to work.
4. Differences in the behavior of females and males reflect "human nature. . . ." (Macionis 1999, 29–30)

Sociologists find that the above four commonsense statements are not true. What concepts are useful for extending sociological knowledge of these statements? To name a few: **Deviance** is a core concept in understanding crime; **social class** is a core concept of sociology in understanding the location of people in the economic structure; **oppression** is a core concept for explaining why some groups, such as the poor, are marginalized in society and are unable to participate in the system of work; and **socialization**, the process of learning the values, norms, and roles of a culture as well as developing a sense of self, is an important concept for understanding how individuals acquire culture.

Our languages are made up of hundreds of thousands of concepts. Chair, table, book, car, status are all concepts. A concept helps us to communicate the idea of car even though cars come in many shapes and sizes. Some concepts have both popular definitions and sociological definitions. For example, the term *norm* is often used as a synonym for *normal*. Used as a sociological concept, norms refer to standards that define expected behaviors. In everyday language, *class* often refers to someone who is sophisticated. Sociologically, *social class* has a different meaning. Max Weber defined social class as based on level of income, wealth, education, occupational prestige, and power. Karl Marx defined social class as a category of people who occupied similar positions in relation to the means of production.

When you create and use a conceptual framework, you will have written a story about what is happening in your community or organization. This will help you link your experiential knowledge with your knowledge gained in the classroom.

PRACTICING SOCIOLOGY USING CRITICAL THINKING

We listed four aspects of practicing sociology in the community at the beginning of this chapter. So far we have discussed the meaning of practicing sociology, the link between practicing sociology and social structure, and using a systematic approach to practicing sociology in a community-based learning program. Next we explore the fourth aspect of practicing sociology: critical thinking. Practicing sociology in the community provides you with a wonderful opportunity for developing critical thinking. You are likely to find that many of your experiences in the community conflict with your own beliefs and values. Your assumptions about social life are being challenged when this happens and, thus, the opportunity to learn is before you. Critical thinking should be an integral part of this learning process. Developing habits of listening, questioning, reading, observing, analyzing, and writing can open your mind to the many possibilities for participating in and learning about social life.

We begin this section by identifying some definitions of critical thinking. Before you read these, write down your own definition of critical thinking. Save it and reevaluate your definition throughout your community-based learning program. Next, we describe in more detail how you can develop the mental habits of listening, questioning, reading, observing, analyzing, and writing. These processes are important aspects of learning critical thinking and bridging the university and the community.

DEFINING CRITICAL THINKING

Critical thinking is an amorphous term. Critics suggest that the term can be too vague or represent such a broad spectrum of actions as to be rendered meaningless. We provide you with a few definitions.

1. "Critical thinking is the stage when ideas are evaluated." (Ruggiero 1996, 11)
2. "Critical thinking is the intellectually disciplined process of actively and skillfully conceptualizing, applying, analyzing, synthesizing, and/or evaluating information gathered from, or generated by, observation,

experience, reflection, reasoning, or communication, as a guide to belief and action." (Scriven and Paul)

3. "Critical thinking is a technique for evaluating information and ideas, for deciding what to accept and believe." (Kurland 2000)

4. "Critical thinking is careful and deliberate determination of whether to accept, reject, or suspend judgment." (Fowler 1996, 3, citing Moore and Parker 1994)

5. Critical thinking is "reasonably and reflectively deciding what to believe or do." (Fowler 1996, 5, citing Ennis 1985)

6. Liz Grauerholz and Sharon Bouma-Holtrop define critical thinking under the term "critical sociological thinking." Accordingly, "critical sociological thinking refers to the ability to logically and reasonably evaluate an argument or problem while maintaining an awareness of and sensitivity to social forces and contexts." (Grauerholz and Bouma-Holtrop 2003, 485)

Return to your own definition of critical thinking. Does it incorporate any aspects of the above definitions? Do you see any similarities in these definitions? Would you challenge any of these definitions? Make notes on your ideas and evaluate them at a future time. We encourage you to read any available literature on critical thinking and discuss what you learn with others.

To encourage you to think about critical thinking, we provide you with a list of characteristics of the ideal critical thinker, including the following:

- Inquisitiveness with regard to a wide range of issues
- Concern to become and remain well-informed
- Alertness to opportunities to use critical thinking
- Trust in the processes of reasoned inquiry
- Self-confidence in one's own abilities to reason
- Open-mindedness regarding divergent world views
- Flexibility in considering alternatives and opinions
- Understanding of the opinions of other people
- Fair-mindedness in appraising reasoning
- Honesty in facing one's own biases, prejudices, stereotypes, or egocentric tendencies
- Prudence in suspending, making, or altering judgments
- Willingness to reconsider and revise views where honest reflection suggests that change is warranted (Facione 1998, 8)

Critical thinking is more than an academic exercise; it is a way of life. More important, this way of life can be learned. Review the list above frequently. Are you developing these characteristics? Have you discovered other characteristics that you think should be added to this list? Further, ask yourself how life might be if people do not use critical thinking. Can you think of some examples from your personal life when someone did not use critical thinking?

DEVELOPING MENTAL HABITS OF CRITICAL THINKING

As part of critical thinking, we have identified some mental habits that you need to possess as you practice sociology in the community. These habits are also essential for developing useful knowledge for you in your personal life. They include **listening**, **questioning**, **reading**, **observing**, **analyzing**, and **writing**.

Listening

Developing good listening habits is important for practicing sociology in the community. "Listening determines what information gets into our world; it actually determines how the world is occurring to us—that is, what it is we define as 'reality'" (Blanke 1998, 65). Listening is important because the culture of any group in the community is embedded in the spoken language of their organization.

There are at least three types of listening: active, reflective, and clarifying.

1. Active listening refers to the process of focusing on the person you are talking to and saying nothing, just listening. This type of listening lets a person know that she or he has your complete attention. It also allows you to mentally record what is being said so that you can record the conversation as soon as possible in your journal.

2. Reflective listening is the process of restating what the person has already said. For example: "I heard you say that. . . ." This process gives the person the opportunity to correct any misunderstandings immediately.

3. Clarifying listening is the process where you get clarification for answers the person has given. For example, you might ask the person to comment further or to clarify certain points. (Lindsay 1996, 253)

Reflecting on these three types of listening may lead you to wonder when each type is used. You will find yourself moving from one type to another throughout the day. Part of carrying out your fieldwork in the community requires that you use active listening. For example, someone in the community will explain to you what the community needs are and what is expected of you. This requires active listening. Since you are also practicing sociology, active listening focuses your attention on the discussion at hand so that you can record pertinent information in your journal as soon as possible after the discussion.

As you notice, however, reflective listening and clarifying listening may also be important as you absorb the information from active listening. You may need to verify what someone has said to you and/or clarify the information. You will find that "good listening" is imperative for having a successful community-based learning program. Good listening can help you practice your sociology and develop critical thinking that requires you "to question, examine, challenge, and propose alternatives to the taken-for-granted social world as they have been taught or told about it" (Strand 1999, 30). Peter Berger and Thomas Luckmann (1966), writing in their book *The Social Construction of Reality*, make this very point when they suggest that sociology is liberating because it helps to reveal taken-for-granted assumptions about the world we live in by acknowledging that reality is socially constructed.

Filters to Listening   What keeps us from listening? You have probably found yourself interacting with someone and thinking to yourself, he isn't listening to a word I say! Or, has someone said to you, "I know I'm right, I heard Mary say those exact words last weekend!" That person may think that she heard something exactly as it was said; however, we all have filters to listening. Here is a list of specific filters to listening (Blanke 1998, 66–77). They are belief in a fixed reality, scripts for how life should go, seeking confirmation and approval, taking everything personally, and already thinking we know that. As you read the following sections on filters to listening, which of these filters are significant in shaping your listening? Eliminating these filters is almost impossible, but you need to be aware of them and how they shape your listening. It is also key to developing critical thinking because to do so you must be aware of your own biases.

Belief in a Fixed Reality

When you filter listening through this belief, you close your mind to all the possibilities in the world. You listen and say, "That's impossible." With this filter, thinking shuts your mind to other possible explanations for social phenomena. In part, we do this because the explanations we accept are useful for us or are the perspective of the organization or group we participate in on a regular basis. For example, the myth still persists that women provoke rape by doing something that leads men to think they want sexual intercourse. This is so even though there is ample evidence to refute this perspective. Practicing sociology means developing a critical approach that questions existing relationships and is sometimes a threat to people who believe they know the truth (Charon 2001). It also means doing something to change the social arrangements that help perpetuate myths and stereotypes.

Scripts for How Life Should Go

This filter refers to placing value judgments on social life. Have you listened to someone and thought to yourself, "That's not the way it should be." In your organization in the community you must be very aware of placing value judgments on what you hear. If you are working in a home for unwed mothers and you hold a strong belief in abstinence before marriage, your script for how life should go will be challenged. You will need to reconsider your values or open up your listening to alternative views to abstinence.

Seeking Confirmation and Approval

Do you ever find yourself thinking about what you are going to say next while someone else is speaking to you? We have probably all done this at one time or another. Through this process we are often seeking approval, "Will they think this is stupid if I say. . . ." One means of reducing the effect of this filter is to be well prepared. For example, if you interview people in your organization, do a thorough job of preparing yourself beforehand for that experience.

Taking Everything Personally

One morning you arrive at your field site and hear two people making lunch plans. You wonder if they are going to invite you along because you have gotten to know them over the past few weeks. Lunchtime comes and they do not ask you to come. Immediately you feel as though they are snubbing you. You might even feel that they no longer like you or like your work. Taking everything personally requires a lot of energy and makes you feel miserable. You must be careful not to construct a world in which you believe you are the focus of everyone else's actions. Sociologically, it reduces your interpretations of social life to the individual level, rather than exploring structural arrangements in society.

Already Thinking We Know That

Have you ever talked to someone who punctuates your entire conversation by saying "I know, I know, I know." Besides being terribly annoying, already thinking we know something closes our minds to the myriad of information out there. You will be challenged throughout your community-based learning program to broaden your knowledge base.

Listening is important for developing critical thinking. As you should see from reading this section, listening has various aspects, and how we listen is complex. Remembering that there are filters to listening can enhance your ability to uncover your own biases.

Questioning

Thinking and learning are not only enhanced by the answers but also by the questions that you ask. Through questioning, you express problems and set the boundaries within which issues are explored. Critical thinking is based on critical questioning, which you can learn to do.

Here are some broad categories of questioning that you can use:

- Raising questions to clarify issues
- Questioning to identify underlying assumptions
- Questions that probe evidence
- Questions related to viewpoint or perspective
- Questions related to implications and consequences of actions
- Questioning the questions (Paul 1990)

To clarify by questioning you may want to have illustrations or examples to help you decide if a statement is accurate. For example, are there data that support the argument that the number of children that are homeless is increasing? You may also want to probe assumptions because assumptions are often implicit in statements or arguments. For example, if you assume that women who have abortions are emotionally scarred for life, this assumption will shape your argument about women's right to abortion in the United States.

Critical questioning also means examining the evidence. Has all available evidence been presented? This includes evidence that may be contrary to a particular argument. Another part of the critical thinking process is questioning whether there are other viewpoints or perspectives that might be useful. Also, what groups might have different perspectives and how do these compare? You must always keep an open mind to alternative perspectives.

Critical questioning also means questioning the implications and consequences of actions. This focuses your attention on evaluation. That is, what are the possible implications of the argument being presented? For example, if you make the argument that people are poor because they are too lazy to work, policies flowing from such an argument would be much different than if you argued that people are poor because of an economic system where work is sometimes limited and wages are frequently too low to allow people to support themselves or their families.

Finally, you need to question the questions. In general, this means that you need to explore why the question being asked is relevant. Further, if you think back to our discussion of paradigms, the paradigm you use helps shape the questions you ask and therefore the answers you get. If you used the functionalist paradigm and your friend used the feminist paradigm to develop questions about violence against women, each of you would address the issue differently and have different questions related to this condition.

Here are some specific questions that you might ask when people are presenting you with information.

- Does the speaker have a bias?
- Has any important evidence been excluded from the speaker's presentation?
- What types of interpretations of the information are possible?
- Has the speaker misstated facts or had errors in reasoning? (Ruggiero 1996, 120–121)

As we mentioned earlier in this chapter, we all have biases. Yet, we do want to know if a person is fair-minded. Are biases made explicit? Regarding evidence, we know that sometimes evidence is excluded inadvertently. Other times, evidence is excluded when it does not support a speaker's position. For example, if a speaker argues that people are homeless because they are too lazy to work, evidence is being excluded because many homeless people do work.

Another important aspect of critical questioning, according to Ruggiero, is being able to identify when evidence is missing. The more you know about a particular issue, the better you are able to do this. Furthermore, all evidence has various interpretations. As we mentioned earlier, it is a fact that some people are poor. Why this is so has many interpretations. You also have to look to see if broad generalizations are made based only on isolated events. Often this is stereotyping groups in society. Also look at how the evidence supports a speaker's assertions. The more you develop your critical thinking the more likely you are to identify errors in reasoning.

We encourage you to practice critical questioning. You can role-play with some of your friends and with classmates. The more experienced you become at critical questioning, the more you will find this type of questioning helpful in your personal life as well as in your course work.

Reading

Critical reading is like any other process involved in critical thinking. Its purpose is to involve you with your experiences (ideas) and observations in such a way that you are able to evaluate them. This takes time and practice. As we discussed earlier, questioning enhances your learning. If you practice asking questions in your reading, you are on the road to developing critical thinking and understanding. To this end, there are several steps in the process of critical reading, noting that these are for presentation only because critical reading is not done in discrete steps.

- Read for literal meaning (decoding the meaning of sentences).
- Analyze and describe (recognize topics and subtopics; classify patterns and their relationships; pay attention to language).
- Interpret an overall meaning (infer meaning and understanding based on how material is presented). (Kurland 2000, 1–2)

So what are the types of questions you should ask to develop your reading? For example, "Where does the author engage in interpretation and/or judgment, as opposed to the simple presentation of factual information? If so, which interpretations and judgments, if any, might reasonably be challenged?" (Ruggiero 1996, 16–17)

You can always gain insights from the work of others. Practicing sociology requires that you read critically what others have written in your area of interest. "Whatever we read with the sociological eye becomes a clue to the larger patterns of society, here or in the past. The same goes for the future" (Collins 1998, 3). Critical reading is important for developing critical thinking as part of practicing sociology. It will help you to explore structural relations in the community.

Observing

We use the concept **critical observation** to refer to the ability to

> (1) recognize the limits of the types of claims one can make about an observation and (2) identify links between individual actions and structural constraints. (Stevens and VanNatta 2002, 245)

Developing the following abilities can enhance critical observation:

1. The ability to recognize the difference between observed behaviors and the meanings we assign to them
2. The ability to identify the assumptions and stereotypes we bring to our interpretations of behaviors

3. Identifying the context in which observations are embedded (Stevens and VanNatta 2002, 245)

Throughout this guide we address these abilities. For example, we mentioned earlier in this chapter that as you work at your field site, you might observe people making lunch plans that exclude you. You must always be aware that there can be many meanings attributed to that observed behavior. In Chapter 3 we discuss stereotypes and how you must discover the assumptions and stereotypes that you hold. Finally, practicing sociology in a community-based learning program entails always trying to put observations in context. Much misinformation is assumed to be fact because this is not done. As we noted earlier in this guide, you cannot understand homelessness by just observing people who do not have homes. Why, in a country as rich in resources as the United States, do people still sleep on the streets? To answer this question, you need to explore social structures that constrain people's choices and opportunities.

Analyzing

Closely linked with critical observation is the process of analyzing your observations and experiences. This process begins with a very basic principle: "It's almost impossible to have an experience without interpreting its meaning" (Blanke 1998, 113). Your interpretations are based on many things, including your own history, your use of language, and the discipline from which you draw your paradigm and conceptual framework. When practicing sociology in the community, try to be systematic in your approach, beginning with some theoretical insights or at least some basic facts.

What is a **fact**? One definition of a fact is an object or event. Another view is that facts are not independent of their social context and thus there are various "truths" to any given event depending on one's perspective. What you think about facts, how you make sense of your data is a matter of analysis and interpretation. It takes reflection to determine if you are talking about facts or your interpretations. That some people in this country are hungry is a fact. That some people in this country are hungry because they are too lazy to work is an interpretation of the fact. That the majority of people in prison are minorities is a fact. Any answer to why this is so is an interpretation.

Interpretation is closely linked with reflection in the process of analysis. Here are a few reasons why reflection is important in learning outside the classroom.

1. Your own experiences are not enough to understand the complexities of social life in the community.
2. Reflection transforms your experiences in the community along with your experiences in the classroom into learning. You benefit from guided reflection.
3. Becoming aware of your own learning through reflection, you also become aware of your own biases. Reflection helps you challenge stereotypes.
4. Reflection becomes an important tool for self-development as well as for later professional development.

Reflection is the link that ties your experiences in the community to academic learning. This means being able to step back and be thoughtful about experience, including monitoring your own reactions and thinking processes (Eyler and Giles 1999, 171). Reflection involves participation. This is not a new idea to you because in your everyday activities you reflect at times on decisions you have made or changes in your life that you did not directly make. Learning in your program takes place when you have experiences in the community, you reflect on these experiences guided by academic learning, and then take action based on your reflections. You must fight the urge to use personal opinion over critical analysis. This is a time for integrating community experiences with your educational experiences.

One way to think about reflection is to consider the following levels of reflection: the Mirror, the Microscope, and the Binoculars (Cooper 1997). The mirror level implies reflection where you focus on yourself; the microscope level requires you to reflect upon your experiences in a community at a more general level; and the binoculars level of reflection suggests that you need to think about what actions you might take to alter social arrangements. We include questions that Mark Cooper provided for you to use in learning how to be reflective. Remember, these levels are created as a means for developing your ability to reflect and do not exist in reality.

The Mirror (a Clear Reflection of the Self)

This level of reflection focuses on the self. Here are some examples of questions you might reflect upon as you practice sociology in a community—questions that focus on who you are. Return to these questions when you are reading the section on "Discovering Yourself" in Chapter 3.

1. Who am I?
2. What are my values?
3. What have I learned about myself through this experience?
4. Do I have more/less understanding or empathy than I did before volunteering [doing an internship, service-learning, or service-learning advocacy]?
5. In what ways, if any, has your sense of self, your values, your sense of "community," your willingness to serve others, and your self-confidence/self-esteem been impacted or altered through this experience?
6. Have your motivations for volunteering [or working for social justice] changed? In what ways?
7. How has this experience challenged stereotypes or prejudices you have/had?
8. Any realizations, insights, or especially strong lessons learned or half-glimpsed?
9. Will these experiences change the way you act or think in the future?
10. Have you given enough, opened up enough, cared enough?
11. How have you challenged yourself, your ideals, your philosophies, your concept of life or the way you live?

The Microscope (Makes the Small Experience Large)

This level of reflection turns your attention to more general aspects of your experiences in a community.

1. What happened? Describe your experiences.
2. What would you change about the situation if you were in charge?
3. What have you learned about this agency, these people, or the community?
4. Was there a moment of failure, success, indecision, doubt, humor, frustration, happiness, sadness?
5. Do you feel your actions had any impact?
6. What more needs to be done?
7. Does this experience compliment or contrast with what you're learning in class? How?

8. Has learning through experience taught you more, less, or the same as the class? In what ways?

The Binoculars (Makes What Appears Distant Appear Closer)

This level of reflection focuses on action and social change.

1. From your service experience, are you able to identify any underlying or overarching issues that influence the problem?
2. What could be done to change the situation?
3. How will this alter your future behaviors/attitudes/and career?
4. How is the issue/agency you're serving impacted by what is going on in the larger political/social sphere?
5. What does the future hold?
6. What can be done?

Use these questions throughout your community-based learning program as a guide for reflecting on who you are, and also for reflecting on your experiences in the community and with social justice.

Writing

Writing—to express, to record, to explain—is an integral part of the thinking and learning process in any discipline (Hylton and Allen 1993, 68). "[W]riting is both a process of doing critical thinking and a product communicating the results of critical thinking" (Bean 1996, 3). Writing provides a way for you to discover and share what is important to you and what you have learned in your community-based learning program.

There are at least three types of writing: *transactional, expressive*, and *poetic* (Bean 1996; Grauerholz 1999, citing Britton et al. 1975). **Transactional writing** has the goals of informing, analyzing, or persuading the reader. Examples include research papers and critiques. This type of writing strengthens critical thinking skills because it requires you to present logical arguments and synthesize ideas. You have probably had the most experience with this type of writing. An important aspect of this type of writing is revising what you have written. As a student, you may find yourself writing a paper for class the night before it is due. You probably know other students who do the same. However, it is important to develop the habit of allowing yourself enough time to rewrite. "Writers produce multiple drafts because the act of writing is itself an act of discovery, or, in Dewey's terms, of 'wrestling with the conditions of the problem' at hand" (Bean 1996, 4).

Expressive writing is reflexive writing and tends to be more informal. It is a way of writing that allows you to take new ideas from a community-based learning site and link them with classroom knowledge. "It is writing to discover and explore, to mull over, to ruminate on, to raise questions about, to personalize" (Bean 1996, 47). Your journal is an example of expressive writing. It is an important type of writing for developing sociological thinking because it requires linking the "personal" and "social world." We discuss this type of writing in Chapter 4, "Recording and Reflecting."

Finally, **poetic writing** is typically what you think of as "creative writing." Examples of poetic writing are fiction and nonfiction writing as well as poetry.

We encourage you to write in as much detail as possible in your journal, as well as in any other products for your course. Writing helps you clarify your thinking. It also becomes the stories that you can share with others. By rewriting, you will have the joy of discovery about your part of your community-based learning program.

CONCLUSION

Practicing sociology in a community-based learning program is an exciting experience that can open your mind to a new and powerful way of looking at the world and understanding social life. "There is literally nothing you can't see in a fresh way if you turn your sociological eye to it. Being a sociologist means never having to be bored" (Collins 1998, 3). Moving beyond your own personal experiences toward an understanding of how social life is created and sustained by systems we all participate in is compelling information for creating social change in the community, transforming yourself, and developing sociological knowledge.

REFLECTIONS

I. DEVELOPING THE SOCIOLOGICAL IMAGINATION (KAUFMAN 1997, 309–314)

We provide you with this exercise for several reasons.

1. It is an opportunity for you to develop your curiosity. For example, most of you have purchased tennis shoes but have you ever thought of tennis shoes as part of a social problem including values as well as economic systems?
2. It provides an opportunity to place issues in their social context.
3. It can help you develop your critical thinking.

Select an object or issue. Peter Kaufman uses Air Jordan basketball shoes. Other items might be cigarettes, computer, diet drug, pink or blue baby blanket, beeper, fast food item, condom, to name a few. You can also use this exercise with issues. For example, mental illness, violence against women, child abuse, drug use, racism, teenage pregnancy, and so on can be explored. This exercise is best done as a group project with some of your classmates.

Write your responses to the questions below so that everyone else can see them. Seeing responses often triggers new responses. Section A helps you to see the importance of describing an object or issue before moving on in your analysis. Section B gives you the opportunity to analyze an object or issue from your own personal biography and the historical context familiar to your life. It will become apparent in this exercise that many of your experiences differ from others doing this exercise. In Section C, you begin to see how local objects or issues are connected to other cultures and societies. Finally, Section D provides you with the opportunity to see how objects and issues change over time, how your own biases affect your interpretations of objects through exploring objects and issues in their historical context. All of these sections help you to develop your sociological imagination and critical thinking. Use this exercise when you are analyzing particular social issues or events in your community-based learning program.

    A. Description

        What is the object under consideration?

        How would you describe it in detail?

        What do you call it?

        How is it referred to?

    B. Local Analysis

        How does it relate to other aspects of social life?

        How is it used, bought, sold?

In what context does it exist?

Who benefits from it?

Who suffers from it?

Why does it appear the way it does?

How does it directly relate to your life?

C. Global Analysis

Does this object exist in other countries? If so, in what form?

How is it used?

How is this use different from its use in the United States?

Is it altered in any way when used elsewhere?

Does it affect life on the planet in any significant way?

Where and how is it made?

D. Historical Analysis

When did the object come into existence?

Why did it appear at this time?

How has the object changed over time?

What other aspects of social life have changed as a result of this object?

How has your use of this object changed over time?

What will this object be like in the future? Will it still exist?

II. DEVELOPING CRITICAL THINKING SKILLS (ADAPTED FROM CHUBINSKI 1996)

We include this exercise as one means of thinking about the social construction of reality as well as an exercise to identify your own biases and assumptions.

Take two minutes to draw a picture of a family. Once everyone involved in this exercise has completed their drawings, share the pictures. Discuss the follow questions:

A. What variations are apparent in the interpretation of a single concept?

B. Why are you likely to find these variations? Do these change over time?

C. How is this exercise useful for recognizing your own assumptions? Why is this important?

D. How might this exercise link to your experiences in the community?

III. VIEWS OF LEARNING

As part of your community-based learning program, you will have many opportunities to learn. As part of critical thinking, it is important that you reflect on how it is that you learn. This is not only important as part of your college experience but is also important when you look for a job, or perform activities of your daily living. Examine these learning styles listed below. Ask yourself which styles are most useful when practicing sociology in a community. Write these down in your journal. Over time, review these learning styles. Have there been any changes in the way you learn?

A. Learning brings about increase in knowledge.

B. Learning is memorizing.

C. Learning is about developing skills and methods, and acquiring facts that can be used as necessary.

D. Learning is about making sense of information, extracting meaning, and relating information to everyday life.

E. Learning is about understanding the world through reinterpreting knowledge. (Kelly 1997)

CHAPTER 3

Exploring
Community Cultures

Beginning your work in the community is an exciting and rewarding time for you, your professor, and those in the community, if your program has been well designed. From your previous work in sociology, you are aware that there are many meanings for community. The term *community* is derived from the Latin word *Communitas* meaning "common or shared." Some people hold that community is shared characteristics such as a similar geographic location, or perhaps same skin color. Others argue that it is shared interests, for example, a community of sociologists, or the local chess club. Yet others view community as **shared culture**, as in norms, values, or roles, such as Americans as a community (Cohen 1992). Sociologists differ as to the degree of consensus that exists over norms, values, or roles in communities. However, most sociologists agree that **culture** consists of the ideas, norms, ideologies, material objects, and techniques that are common to members of a particular social group. Sociologist William Du Bois writes a particularly descriptive definition of culture.

> Culture is a set of shared meanings. It is the definitions of the situation, the vision, the stories, the folklore, the shared understandings, the language, the material artifacts, the rules and policies, the norms, the theme/mood, and the ethos. (1997, 46)

Culture and structure are inexplicitly linked, with social structure organizing the ideas we hold about reality into "social relationships that connect people to one another and to systems as well as connecting entire systems to one another" (Johnson 1997, 80–81). When you are practicing sociology in a community, you are likely to see some differences among groups based on these ideas of culture.

In this chapter we begin by exploring the importance of culture in a community-based learning program. Keep asking yourself how you are shaped by the cultures you participate in during your community-based learning program. Next, we describe the distinction between symbolic and material culture. We follow this by a discussion of organizational culture and how it exhibits both symbolic and material culture. Finally, we address how and why a community-based learning program can help you discover yourself. This includes uncovering your values, assumptions, beliefs, biases, and stereotypes.

THE IMPORTANCE OF CULTURE

Culture is conveyed within generations and from one generation to another through the process of socialization. Culture is a social process. Human beings are exceptional in their ability to reflect upon the culture within which they reside and challenge existing social arrangements.

Why is culture important to you? In general, during your community-based learning program, you are likely to learn about new cultures. Through interactions with others, people create cultures that work for them (Charon 2001). There are at least four reasons why this is so, according to Joel Charon.

1. *First, individuals take on perspectives that work for them.* As you begin practicing sociology in the community, you are likely to be part of a group that has a perspective that is comfortable for you. In general, individuals select groups with perspectives they like and stay away from those groups where they feel uncomfortable.

2. *Second, interaction reinforces the culture one is participating in.* The more you interact with people at your field site, the more likely you will be to accept the group's perspective as the most useful. In this way certain perspectives become reaffirmed and you are creating culture. This process can hinder critical thinking.

3. *Third, the reason an individual takes on the perspective of the group is that the group encourages conformity through sanctions and rewards.* For example, if you continue to arrive late for work, you will probably receive negative sanctions. If you go beyond what is expected of you, you may receive positive sanctions, perhaps a letter of commendation from the organization to your university.

4. *Fourth, individuals come to believe in the perspective or culture of the group because their beliefs are shared with others in the group.* Standing alone with our beliefs is extremely difficult. (Charon 2001, 109–110)

You are more likely to avoid **ethnocentrism,** judging other cultures by the standards of your own culture, through a better understanding of how your interactions with others create a culture or shared perspective about social reality. Ethnocentrism can lead to treating people differently or making choices about alternatives that might lead to inequalities and oppression for some groups in society.

It is culture that shapes your reality about the world. Cultures are inclusive; once you become part of a community there are cultural forces to make you be like the rest of the group. Inclusion brings with it a form of privilege. To be white in the

United States is supported by racist culture, including norms that maintain white dominance (Gillespie 2003; McIntosh 1988). Some of our students provided the following examples of what it means to have white privilege: "If you are white, you are less likely to be stopped by police if you are driving in a neighborhood late at night." "To be white means that you will not be asked if you were given special consideration to get into college." "If you are white, you are also less likely to be with people who are different from you. This includes interacting with teachers, lawyers, and physicians." When white people are treated differently based solely on the group they belong to, "then social privilege is at work" (Johnson 1997, 28).

Cultures are also exclusive. If people do not conform to group values, beliefs, and norms, they may be excluded from the group. For example, gays and lesbians are excluded from military service if they state their sexual orientation; women are largely excluded from top-level positions in industry; and people of color have historically been excluded from restaurants, hotels, schools, workplaces, and churches. How are cultures constructed? In the next section we explore this complex process.

CONSTRUCTING CULTURES

The social world in which we live is made up of both nonmaterial (symbolic) and material cultures. For example, we can look at music and see how it contains ideas of both symbolic and material cultures (Johnson 1997). On the one hand, musical notes represent the music you hear on a CD (compact disc). Music is expressed symbolically through notes and sounds that humans make and interpret. On the other hand, there is also a material aspect to music. You probably own CDs and have a CD player, or have an instrument that you play. CDs are physical objects made by members of a society that shape people's lives. CDs and CD players have offered people the opportunity to listen to their music in more locations, for example, when jogging or while driving a car. This is just one example of the interplay between symbolic and material culture. When practicing sociology at your community-based learning site, keep notes on other examples of the duality of culture. Sociologically, it is important to see how symbolic and material cultures, together, shape social life.

Within communities or organizations, you are unlikely to find just one shared culture. Discovering the various cultures means exploring the extent of shared values, learning about people's assumptions concerning their community or organization, and uncovering their reflections and interpretations about their community or organization. Identifying and analyzing these differences is one means of exploring power relationships within communities or organizations. It provides one way to look at social change (Ristock and Pennell 1996).

Richard Paul and Linda Elder identify some questions that you could ask about organizational realities. Here are a few examples from this list of questions.

- To what extent is there a struggle for power underway within the organization?
- What is the hierarchy of power in the organization? To what extent are those at the top easily threatened by thinking that diverges from their own?
- To what extent is there a problem of bureaucratic inefficiency within the organization?
- To what extent is there a problematic "ideology" that stands in the way of change?
- To what extent are ethical considerations ignored or denied in favor of vested interest within the organization? (2002)

Paul and Elder suggest that you think through these questions and focus them on the organization where you are working.

Next we look at symbolic culture and its significance. We do the same for material culture. We also examine organizational culture, showing how it encompasses both symbolic and material cultures. Some of you are likely to carry out your community-based learning program in an organization or agency.

SYMBOLIC CULTURES

Human beings are cultural (Charon 2001). The essence of their being is the ability to use symbols to understand their world. "Symbols make cultures possible because they're what we use to give something meaning beyond what it otherwise 'is'" (Johnson 1997, 39). You give names to things, for example, car, condom, beer, or dorm. By naming some things, these become part of your culture and they shape relationships. You become connected. You construct reality by giving names to things, and those things that are unnamed are outside of your reality.

Written and spoken language, a system of symbols, is probably the best example of the use of symbols creating culture. Through language we create and learn cultural values, norms, ideologies, and so on. Human beings also develop their sense of self, based largely on symbolic cultures.

Significance of Symbolic Culture

Sociologically, symbols help us give meaning to events and through this process we enter into relationships. Both written and spoken language is an important aspect of symbolic culture. Some argue that storytelling "constitutes the heart of cultural survival" (Fine and Weis 1998, 208). It is through storytelling that many cultures have passed their cultures on to the next generation. Storytelling may become an important data source for you during your community-based learning program.

Exploring the idea of symbolic culture is also significant because ideas about values, norms, and ideologies are linked with understanding social control. Values become our starting point for judging others. Our values are our ideas about what is right or good in society. Norms become a way of exerting social control to insure that people conform. Closely linked is the idea of ideologies. Ideologies often justify the use of power and its outcome, as we discuss in the following text in relation to poverty and racism.

We cannot see symbolic culture, such as values, beliefs, or ideology. Material culture includes what we can see, for example, documents or physical structures; however, these aspects of material culture do not have meaning without their symbolic aspects. For example, a classroom has no meaning until we pay attention to the values and beliefs associated with learning in this society.

Aspects of Symbolic Culture

Some of the most important ideas about symbolic cultures and how they shape human thinking, behavior, and action are embodied in the concepts of values, norms, language, and ideology. People and social groups participating in social systems make these concepts meaningful.

Values   "Private universities are better than public ones." "Gay unions are better than straight marriages." "The death penalty should be used for certain types of crimes." "Internships are better than service action programs." These statements all express values. However, this does not mean that these statements are right. Values contain *assumptions* about how the world *should be;* they are judgments, not facts. We learn values through socialization, and they shape how we see and interpret our social world. Values influence our choices and shape how we "perceive and treat ourselves and other people" (Johnson 1997, 49).

Values are culturally defined standards of what is desirable, good, and just. From some sociological paradigms like functionalism, the focus is on culture characterized by shared values. Other paradigms, for example conflict or feminism, are more likely to focus on values as being in conflict or oppressive to some while helping others. Yet other paradigms, for example symbolic interactionism, focus more on their meanings and how values shape social interactions. As we noted in Chapter 2, the concepts you use and how you apply them in research in your community-based learning program are shaped by the sociological paradigm that guides your research.

Values enter your social life when you begin to make judgments concerning others. They are reinforced in society by institutions like the media, schools, religion, and the workplace. Identify some of the values in your organization. Does everyone share these values? If not, it may be useful to explore how values are embedded in social institutions and thus shape social arrangements. Record this information in your journal. See if your analysis of values in your organization changes over time.

Often you make choices about possible alternatives based on the values and preferences you hold for how to make the world a better place. As you continue to interact with others, cultural patterns form, you get used to these patterns, and ultimately these patterns make up your social world. You experience values as a natural part of reality, not as things that are socially constructed. Your values are largely learned through socialization and are powerful in shaping what you believe, how you act, and how you feel.

Because you are a part of what you study, it is important to apply critical thinking skills to the practice of sociology as you discover the social forces, created and reinforced by human action, that shape social life. Such discovery is challenging because what you find is often in conflict with your commonly held assumptions about social reality and how it is organized. For example, many people in society value equality of opportunity. Yet research indicates that inequalities in educational opportunities are increasing in the United States, as is the disparity between the rich and the poor.

Shaping your own values is part of a community-based learning program because reflection is an intentional activity of thinking about and connecting your learning experiences in the community with your educational experiences. With this process you have the opportunity to integrate these experiences into your own value system.

Norms Practicing sociology in the community can initiate feelings of excitement, fear, apprehension, and so on. As you participate in the system of work and cultures of an organization, you will quickly find that the system affects how you think, feel, and behave as a participant. For example, how you dress, your work behavior, how you interact with others, and how you feel about yourself are all part of your cultural experiences. There may seem to be so many things that you can do, should do, and want to do. You will probably soon see that there are many **norms** (shared rules that govern behavior) shaping your behavior at your field site. The longer you are in a community or organization the more you will be able to identify the behavior expected of you in particular situations.

When you are working in a community, you are probably in a new environment, the norms of behavior may not be clear, you are likely to be confronted with situations that you may not be fully prepared to handle, and you may react with a variety of emotions. In Chapter 4 we ask you to record these emotions in your journal. One way to make sense of these feelings is to apply the concept of **emotional labor** (what workers do with their feelings to comply with organizational norms or rules of behavior) (Hochschild 1983; Yanay and Shahar 1998). This concept may also be useful for helping you understand how you fit into the power structure at your field site. It is a valuable concept for unearthing and analyzing the subtle **social control** (various means by which conformity to norms is encouraged) of organizations.

The feminist paradigm led to the development of the concept of *emotional labor,* a concept that helps explain how people's lives can be controlled in the workplace:

> Employers require workers to manipulate their own feelings as part of their job . . . how we act in certain ways, display certain facial or body gestures, and feel certain feelings, all in the line of duty. In essence, we exchange our emotions for wages. (Lori Holyfield 1997, 243, citing Hochschild 1983)

Others suggest that emotional labor refers to "what workers do with their feelings to comply with organizational role requirements" (Yanay and Shahar 1998, 346). Emotional labor is a means of developing a professional identity, which is often separated from one's personal identity and is shaped by the organization. The authors, Niza Yanay and Golan Shahar, use the example of a third-year psychology student who worked in a shelter for chronic mental patients and was called a "fat whore" by one of these patients. Rather than getting angry, the student responded to organizational role requirements by remaining calm and changing negative feelings into pity. Yanay and Shahar argue that, within the work setting, it is the structure of work that shapes how emotional labor, workers' feelings, are suppressed, expressed, or transformed.

The following example is a way to understand emotional responses to events by applying the concept of emotional labor. Put yourself in the place of an intern who decided to work in a hospital as part of her internship experience. You are asked to follow a physician into a patient's room to observe the interaction between the doctor and her patient. Upon entering the room, the physician acknowledges the patient and asks him, "Why are you here?" The patient exclaims, "Get her out of here." You had not had a patient ask you to leave before and you feel very uncomfortable and self-conscious, and your feelings are hurt. You leave the room without saying anything. When the physician finally comes out of the patient's room, she tries to explain to you what happened and why the patient did not want you there. She tells you that it was not your fault. But you feel excluded, incompetent, and like an outsider. However, you tell the physician that everything is fine and nothing is bothering you. This is a situation in which you could apply the concept of emotional labor. This concept could be useful for examining the processes of how social control within the hospital can shape emotional responses. Think about how the hospital structure might affect people's actions in a hospital setting. Imagine how you would feel if you experienced this interaction. In this example, the norms or rules of proper behavior in social interaction with a patient or with a physician have not been challenged.

There are several questions you might ask related to emotional labor at your field site. Record these answers in your journal. In addition, it may be informative to discuss your experiences with others in the classroom.

1. How is this organization intervening in my emotional life?
2. How does the organization generate what it defines as appropriate emotional responses? That is, what emotional responses are acceptable to the organization?
3. Does emotional labor shape the way I feel about myself?

Language   **Language** is perhaps the key to creating, sustaining, and changing culture. Language is a symbolic system of verbal and sometimes written representations by which symbols are linked together to form ideas with shared meanings about a culture. During your participation in the community, you may do "discourse analysis," meaning "analysis that examines languages and ideologies as a way of understanding how meanings are produced" (Ristock and Pennell 1996, 114). Such an analysis could help you understand how communities or organizations are controlled through cultures (Ristock and Pennell 1996, citing Witten 1993).

A student in our community-based learning program participated in a labor movement in which immigrants were attempting to organize a union in a hostile environment. She writes the following:

> One of their [the workers] main chants signified "we are the union, the mighty, mighty union." Another chant [was], "Se se puede; yes we can."

This student analyzes how this language provides meanings for the general public to understand and hear the purposes of the union. She also argues that this language creates meaning for the group: Only together can they make their lives better.

The power of language is often left unexplored; however, the use of language and who controls it has a major influence on how cultures are organized and sustained.

> Culture shapes language, and language fosters or facilitates many aspects of thought. . . . The concepts and categories learned as children shape how we experience the world around us, and these concepts and categories—including stereotypes and prejudices—are usually delineated in sets of words and phrases. (Feagin 2001, 119)

For example, whites still use epithets regarding African Americans, especially when they are not in public. Use of derogatory language is just one example of how language structures everyday life for everyone in society. It shapes our beliefs about people and, in this instance, helps to sustain racism in American society.

The use of language can also exclude and alienate people in society. For example, according to Johnson (1997, 45) a century ago the word "homosexual" referred only to a person's sexual orientation. More recently words like "gay," "lesbian," or "heterosexual" refer to a person's identity and therefore are used to place people into distinct groups or categories. These differences form the basis for inequalities with heterosexuals privileged over other groups.

Young (1990) concurs when she argues that not respecting the differences of groups that are in variance from the dominant groups in society leads to injustices and exclusion, which she refers to as oppression. Young further argues that the identities of groups, which come out of lived experiences, are important and are the foundation for empowering groups to create social change.

Language also plays an important role in gender socialization. Women are more likely than men to be described by their sexuality. One study "found 220 English words used to negatively describe sexually active women, but only 22 describing sexually active men" (Neubeck and Glasberg 1996, 155). The use of certain language reinforces the institutionalization of domination and oppression in American society.

Ideology **Ideology** is a system of ideas that legitimates existing structural inequalities in a culture, usually developed and maintained by privileged groups in society. Here is an example of how ideologies help to legitimate and sustain poverty. According to Feagin and Feagin (1990), the U.S. government has many subsidy programs, several of which provide government aid for the middle and upper classes. One system of subsidies includes the following: agricultural subsidies, tax credits and tax relief for corporations, subsidies provided to manufacturers of aircraft and pharmaceuticals, to name some. The list goes on, but what is important here is that these subsidies benefit mainly the middle and upper classes. Another system of subsidies is directed at the poor. This system includes: Medicaid, Aid for Families with Dependent Children (now called the Temporary Assistance for Needy Families program, which replaced AFDC and Job Opportunities and Basic Skills Training programs), food stamps, the Head Start Program, and public housing, to name some.

Feagin and Feagin (1990) go on to say that the former subsidy system directed primarily at the middle and upper classes is usually thought of as beneficial and not viewed as "welfare." The latter subsidy system, primarily directed at the poor, is typically thought of by policymakers and the public in unfavorable terms and viewed as providing "handouts to the poor." However, tax exemptions for businesses, home ownership, and other deductions and exemptions for corporations and wealthy individuals amount to far more in the federal budget than the cost of support for the poor.

Subsidy systems shape everyday lives. They justify the political and economic systems in this country by legitimating the class structure. They rely on the ideology that individualism is the key to being successful and the poor have only to want to work, even when their poverty is rooted in structural issues such as unemployment, racism, and classism. This ideology has, in part, shaped the current welfare laws in the United States and helps to maintain the status quo.

Racist ideology is also a social force in America (Feagin 2001). Racist "frameworks" are generally created and maintained by the powerful in society. For example, there is the widely accepted ideology that a black person has equal opportunities in this society. Both blacks and whites hold this ideology, which benefits those elites who want to maintain the status quo. When such an ideology is embedded in the structure of society, attempts to reduce discrimination and oppression are met with resistance, because many people believe that racism no longer exists in the United States (Feagin 2001).

Ideologies function to make the ideas of the privileged in society appear universal. Thus, they are components of power relations and are of interest in many forms of advocacy. Because ideologies inform both social and political actions, they are an integral part of public issues and must be applied when practicing sociology in the community. It is important to give yourself reflective space in order to explore the system of ideas that legitimate existing social arrangements in society and thus create inequalities and oppression in communities. It is not easy to study that of which you are a part and which has an effect on shaping how you think, act, and feel. The community you are in provides you with a wealth of experiences, issues, and ideologies that you can explore through practicing sociology.

Finally, as part of your community-based learning program, how might you identify your own ideologies or explore the ideologies of others? We believe that reflection is an important process that will allow you to identify, examine, and interpret your ideas about the "way things should be." This is not easy because critical reflection requires you to think about the way you think. To explore the ideologies of others you must apply critical thinking and reflection and use your sociological imagination.

In addition to constructing symbolic cultures, culture is also made possible by constructing a material reality. Material cultures, created by humans, shape your participation in social systems.

MATERIAL CULTURE

Material culture consists of all the physical objects, including tools, technology, cities, places of worship, dress, art, movies, and so on that shape the lives of people who live in a particular society. Rossman and Rallis give several specific examples of material culture.

> These might include objects, such as children's schoolwork or photographs . . . but are typically documents—the written record of a person's life or an organization's functioning. Journals, diaries, minutes of meeting, policy statements, letters, and announcements are all examples of material culture. . . . Archival data are another example of material culture. These are the routinely gathered records of a society, community, or organization—for example, attendance records, test scores, and birth and death records. . . . (1998, 145–146)

Once you identify items of material culture, you need to interpret their meanings, being mindful that meanings do not reside with the objects themselves. To illustrate: You and I go see a movie together. We both enjoy the movie, but we come away with different ideas of what the movie is trying to portray. In part, this is because we have different histories. We may come from different cultures and have different experiences that shaped who we are. These past experiences will also shape how we interpret the movie. **Interpretation** refers to "bring[ing] to bear our existing knowledge of the social and cultural circumstances" (Cottle 1997, 284) to make sense of our observations and experiences. We also have to be careful because interpretation is affected by our biases. What questions could you ask to learn more about movies? Using a critical sociological approach, you might question what is being portrayed in movies. Do the movies represent a particular class or group's values? Are some groups in movies portrayed in a stereotypical way? Similar to analyzing movies, other objects of material culture at your field site offer a myriad of opportunities for you to exercise your sociological imagination while practicing sociology in the community.

Significance of Material Culture

It is important to analyze material culture in order to explore social stratification and social conflict. It is also important to be aware of how material culture shapes choices and ultimately how we think about things. "We create it [material culture] and make it part of our identities, and yet we often experience it as separate and external—autonomous and powerful in relation to ourselves" (Johnson 1997, 75). That is, we create material culture that we depend on, for example, walls in buildings, organizational charts, cell phones, fax machines, computers, videophones, written laws, but we forget that they are things that people have made.

Yet these items, along with many others, are often used as a means of social control. "We have to see where material culture fits in a social system, how people perceive, value, and think about it, and what they do with it" (Johnson 1997, 74). Having access to certain objects, like fax machines, can make a difference and create options. For example, human rights issues became more widely known when Chinese students were faxing information to the world about what was going on in Tiananmen Square in 1989. Another example of material culture is the media: newspapers, books, magazines, television, and so on. How has the media, for example, shaped our understanding of wars, women, religion, or the poor and poverty in this society and globally? Your knowledge about particular aspects of social life may be challenged. Some of you will find that what you think you know is wrong.

Aspects of Material Culture

One means for distinguishing material culture from symbolic culture is to think about it in terms of documents and artifacts (Cottle 1997). People make material culture through their interactions with others and with the physical world. Aspects of material culture are most often linked with aspects of symbolic culture. It is the latter that gives meaning to material cultures.

Documents   Documents are typically thought of as written records that sociologists use as a resource. These documents contain or store information. More broadly, documents can also be thought of as material objects that represent something. For example, the *Congressional Record* is a document that reports and records information. But it is more than that. It not only tells us some of what goes on in Congress, but it can also tell us what information is added to the record, as well as that which is missing. It can also be a resource for seeing how elites carry out parts of their political life.

Organizational charts, policy manuals, public relations materials, bulletin board displays, memos, faxes, e-mails, Internet, advertising, telephone books are all of value to sociologists who wish to understand community cultures. According to Simon Cottle, "Documents do not simply report and record; they also *represent*" [italics in text] (1997, 284). He provides an example of a patient's medical record:

> [A]s well as telling us something about this particular person's medical history, [a patient's record] can tell us about the sort of information that is collected, stored and used by doctors and even about the sort of society that encourages such documentation. (1997, 284)

This example illustrates that documents not only provide you with text to analyze, but also give you the opportunity to "use your sociological imagination to recover aspects of their social context that those who produced the document may never have intended or even thought about" (Cottle 1997, 284).

Artifacts   Artifacts are "any produced material object that has become invested with meaning and therefore become part of material culture" (Cottle 1997, 286). For example, the functional purpose of walls is typically to protect people and property from others or from the weather. Cottle goes on to say that walls are invested with diverse social meanings: "Walls make our social space, territories and social distinctions of social power, wealth, and status" (1997, 287). High walls surrounding a mansion may demonstrate wealth and exclusivity while prison walls mark the general undesirability of prison inmates to the community. In this sense, walls are imbued with social meanings and these meanings depend on where you find yourself. In office buildings today there are walls of varying sizes and shapes, from low cubical walls to large, hard wall offices with many windows and total privacy. The possible interpretations of these walls can be varied. An analysis of walls illustrates this point. If you work within a building, walls surround you. What are their meanings? What are their origins, purposes, and uses? Under what conditions were they produced? What do people put on their walls? What are some consequences of these walls for participants in the organization? Write a short essay in which you use critical thinking to explore the "meaning of walls" in your organization.

Many of you are likely to do a community-based learning program in an organization. Next we discuss organizational cultures and how these cultures embody both symbolic and material cultures.

ORGANIZATIONAL CULTURES: AN EXAMPLE

As you practice sociology in the community, be mindful of the relationships between symbolic and material culture. In the following text we provide you with examples of the relationships between symbolic and material cultures in organizations. Studies of organizational culture may cover interpretations of

> formal policies, structures, informal practices, rituals, and organizational stories as well as extensive descriptions of the physical environments in which people worked. (Martin 2001)

When we study cultures, we are concerned with what people do, what people know, and the things people make and use. These learned and shared aspects of human experience are described as cultural behavior, cultural knowledge, and cultural artifacts (Spradley 1980). We know that culture is not observed directly. While cultural knowledge is not obvious, it is very important because we all use it to generate behavior and interpret our experience. In the following text, we use the example of organizations to highlight the cultural behavior, cultural knowledge, and cultural artifacts that make up symbolic and material cultures as described previously.

Organizational cultures hold a wealth of examples of symbolic culture. As we have previously discussed, symbolic culture, in the form of language, is a powerful source for influencing how you think, feel, and behave. For example, if you visit someone in the hospital you may hear a new language over the intercom. Words like "code red," "code blue," and "code white" are used in some hospitals. Code red means a fire, code blue means that someone is dying, and code white warns of a baby abduction. This example illustrates how hospitals use language to create culture. Meanings are given to this language. For example, a code blue sets in action many responses by people who work in hospitals. If you have experienced this particular cultural language, how did it make you feel, act, or behave?

Another example comes from sociologist George Ritzer (2000) who wrote a book entitled *The McDonaldization of Society.* He has also written several articles and been interviewed many times. You may want to read, in more detail, his argument of *McDonaldization* and apply your critical thinking skills and critical reflection to evaluate his arguments.

Focusing on the organization of fast-food restaurants, Ritzer argues that the processes that dominate fast-food restaurants are becoming the dominant processes in the rest of society as well. Organizational cultures include many values and ideologies. According to Ritzer, "McDonaldization" has five dimensions or "rationalization principles" (efficiency, calculability, predictability, control through technology, and replacement of human by nonhuman labor) that have limited worker and consumer choices in fast food restaurants (Ritzer 2002, 7; 2000). Efficiency refers to the most effective means of production; calculability refers to those things that can be counted or quantified; predictability refers to the organization of production; and control through technology and replacement of humans by nonhuman labor, two elements that are closely linked according to Ritzer, refer to substituting nonhuman labor for human labor through the use of technology, often to increase control.

Ritzer argues that workers in McDonald's do not have the opportunity to use their creative talents because their behavior is constrained by the organizational structure of the restaurant. The amount of Coke going into a cup is measured. Hamburgers are made a certain way. According to Ritzer, consumer behavior is also constrained. Consumers become unpaid workers who fill their own drink cups and bus their tables. Although it appears that McDonald's is cheap food for the consumer, it is also cheap for the organization to prepare and sell, thus continuing to generate profits for the stockholders while paying nearly minimum wage for its workers.

The appearance of a "universal culture" of McDonald's also leads to the elimination of differences in eating experiences. As many of you know, McDonald's restaurants look very similar in building style (material culture) as well as in organization, whether you are in Virginia, Florida, California, or another country. How many of you have traveled to a new city or country and gone to McDonald's to eat because it made you feel comfortable, you knew what to expect, and you knew the norms of behavior?

Along with symbolic culture, material aspects of organizational cultures also shape behavior and generate social conflict. People create material culture, change it, and yet tend to forget that it is integral to who they are and the choices they have in life. Documents are evidence of the material culture of an organization. You may find that there are many documents to collect in your organization. For example, brochures, strategic planning documents, and material on Web sites might be of interest. Other documents might include promotion policies, termination policies, and other formal and informal practices.

There will be times when supporting documents and visual data may be important to your field research. For example, it may be useful to have a copy of the organizational chart and the mission of the organization in which you are observing. You may not be aware of the importance of the organization mission and most likely would not know where to find it. Some large, complex organizations, like universities, may have missions at several levels in the structure. For example, the sociology department will have a mission; the school of Arts and Sciences, or the college that administers all liberal arts departments will have a mission; and the university at the presidential level will have a mission for the entire organization. The mission generally states the impact the organization plans to have on its members and sometimes on the outside community. We suggest it would be useful to know the types of occupations within the organization, as well as the proposed budget. These are all text-based documents.

There are also nontext-based documents for you to collect in an organization. If you are in a social service organization, videos might be a nontext-based document for data on your topic of interest. Graphic representations may also be useful. When you are doing field studies, the types of documents you collect are based on their availability. Sometimes the type of document available is not exactly what you would like. Other times one type of document, for example a nontext-based document, can help to clarify information from a text-based document.

Seeing how different aspects of social life fit together is an important part of practicing sociology in the community. Reflecting on our previous examples, you see that symbolic and material cultures are not discrete but rather are intimately connected. For example, rationalization principles that exist in the fast food industry are made possible by the technology, a material aspect of culture that is available to achieve rationalization. To illustrate, food can be frozen and put on the grill and cooked almost immediately, drink machines can premeasure the amount of soda to dispense, and paper products can store and serve as containers for the limited number of products that are sold. In another example, walls, as part of material culture, hold many symbolic meanings. They can mean power, privilege, and oppression, among other things. These various meanings come through interpretations that are often based on context, personal interest, and values, to name a few.

For those of you practicing sociology in an organization or agency, exploring the cultural aspects of your organization might lead you toward the following:

- Analyzing the meanings of cultural manifestations (interpretations are likely to vary)
- Analyzing material cultural manifestations and how these are made possible by symbolic manifestations
- Highlighting cultural norms in an organization
- Interpreting the formal policies, rituals, or storytelling in the organization (Martin 2001)

These and many other cultural aspects of organizations can provide you with the opportunity to broaden your own perspective, challenge your views of social reality, explore future career choices, and become an advocate for social justice. In the next section, we talk about taking the path of greater resistance to create social change. In Chapter 6 we give you more specific strategies for becoming an advocate for social justice.

TRANSFORMING CULTURES

Culture provides you with options for living. Although sociologists identify patterns of behavior, we do not all act in the same way. Some of you are more likely to accept the status quo while others of you try to change existing social arrangements. That is, some of you follow the path of least resistance, while others take the path of greater resistance. We should note that depending on circumstances, you might choose one path over the other.

You are likely to follow the **path of least resistance** for practicing sociology at your field site, meaning that you will "play by the rules" or follow the norms. That is, you are likely to do what is expected of you in your position. Following the path of least resistance is one measure of maintaining the status quo. Most of you will follow the norms of behavior reinforced by the cultures of the community.

But what happens if the norms at your field site conflict with your personal beliefs or the expected behaviors identified by your university? Conflicting paths of least resistance can create role conflict. You are then faced with choices about how to participate. While your choices may seem endless, the culture in which you participate lays out the possible options (Johnson 1997).

As you participate in a community or organization, your options may be limited by the following: gender, age, race/ethnicity, sexual orientation, class, type of organization you are participating in, country you live in, and so on. You are likely to be so accustomed to participating as a person of a particular ethnicity, gender, sexual orientation, and so on, that you must look critically at how your options to make different choices are constrained by your statuses. You must give yourself reflective space; that is, room to think critically about your observations and experiences in the community as well as linking these to your classroom experiences.

Taking the path of greater resistance is your opportunity to transform society. Social change has to reside in changing the structural arrangements in society that are shaped by cultures. You can always choose paths of greater resistance or create them. However, in order to do this, you must be aware of how you are connected to the systems that you participate in. One way to develop this awareness is through taking courses in sociology and applying what you have learned to your personal life. Part of this learning process is understanding that more than your desire to do some things and not to do others shapes your participation in life. You must look to your values and beliefs and examine them with a critical eye. For example, your status as a man or women, rich or poor, white or a person of color all affect your experiences in the educational system, political system, economic system, and so on. But you cannot understand how you are connected to these systems until you make the further connection between culture and social structure. Cultural beliefs, values, language, and ideologies are all embedded in structures with the consequence that not all groups have equal opportunities. For example, if you are poor your opportunity to attend college is constrained. If you are a woman, you are less likely to be in a leadership role in Congress. If you are a person of color, you are less likely to participate fully in the health care system. Describe at least one interaction where you perceived you were limited by one or more of your statuses. Keep a running account of these instances in your journal.

The **path of greater resistance** is grounded in the idea of empowerment. Young refers to empowerment as "participation of an agent in decision making through an effective voice and vote" (Young 1990, 251). Another definition of empowerment fits very closely with the ideas of service-learning advocacy discussed in this guide.

> Empowerment is a consequence of liberatory learning. Power is not given, but created within the emerging praxis in which co-learners are engaged. The theoretical basis for this discovery is provided by critical consciousness: Its expression is collective action on behalf of mutually agreed upon goals. Empowerment is distinct from building skills and competencies, these being commonly associated with conventional schooling. Education for empowerment further differs from schooling both in its emphasis on groups (rather than individuals) and its focus on cultural transformation (rather than social adaptation). (Heaney 1995, 12)

This definition is generally consistent with our discussion of practicing sociology in a service-learning advocacy program in the community. It highlights the importance of faculty, students, and community members, as learners, working together to challenge existing social structures that dominate and exploit certain groups in a community. This learning takes place through collectively struggling and attempting to interpret problems using critical thinking.

Taking the path of greater resistance can be challenging but rewarding. For those of you who are participating in advocacy work, taking the path of greater resistance is often necessary for creating a more just society. Here are two examples of people practicing sociology and taking the path of greater resistance by doing research grounded in social advocacy (Feagin and Vera 2001, 186–191).

The first example is of a group of sociologists in Milwaukee, Wisconsin, working with an inner-city group, the Fair Lending Coalition, to effect change in banks' practices of investing in the inner city. Historically, in Milwaukee, banks tended to reject blacks more often than whites for home and small business loans. These sociologists, working closely with the community, were able to document this disparity and enabled the Coalition to challenge banks to change their lending practices.

In another example, sociologists working with local community groups in Houston, Texas, used their research skills to find the patterns of waste distribution in the area. They found that most incinerators and landfills were in areas of the city where blacks lived. Using these data, a group called the Northeast Community Action Group was able to change the way permits for waste distribution were made, thus restricting the future location of waste facilities.

As you can see from these examples, sociologists worked with community members in a collaborative manner. In addition, they went against the generally held norms, beliefs, and ideologies that had previously created inequalities and oppression, such as unequal access to loans based on the color of one's skin.

Paths of least resistance or greater resistance are defined by the context in which they occur. Making choices about taking the path of least resistance or greater resistance is structured, in part, by the cultures in which you participate. Thus, when practicing sociology in the community or in your daily life, a critical sociological approach, using critical thinking and critical reflection, should help you to uncover and question existing social structures and cultures. This should give you the opportunity to question and analyze the status quo and make more informed choices.

In the next section, we explore the process of discovering yourself. Many community-based learning programs have as one of the commitments of the program to educate students about discovering their own identity. In part, this can be done through exposing students to different groups of people in the community as well as providing them the opportunities to challenge stereotypes.

DISCOVERING YOURSELF

If you have not been active in community work in the past, it is likely that you will feel some trepidation as you begin this new journey. Have you heard a student say, "I arrived at my field site and no one was waiting for me, there were no written plans for what I should do. I didn't even have a place to sit!" If you feel this way when you begin practicing sociology in the community, you may be experiencing what sociologists describe as **culture shock,** meaning you are encountering new and different cultures that may disrupt your normal assumptions about social values and practices. However, you can make this an important experience for yourself.

> Perhaps the greatest service sociology can offer to its students is to teach them to understand the ways in which what they perceive to be their "personal troubles" may in fact be "public issues," how their own biographies—their loves, their demons—are oftentimes those of many others. Even more importantly, once the student understands his or her connection to "others,"

to social structure, he or she understands the ways in which that structure both creates those demons and how that structure might be changed to alleviate them. (Goodwin 1997, 28)

The existence of culture is powerful in shaping you as an individual and participant observer in the community. Thus, you need to reflect upon the importance of culture as you begin practicing sociology in the community, trying as best you can to know yourself. Your history, values, beliefs, and so on are those qualities you bring to the community that are formed and shaped by cultures. In his book entitled *Mind, Self and Society* (1934), George Herbert Mead identifies the uniqueness of human beings because of the way they can use symbols such as language to communicate and think, and also because of their ability to be reflective. Individuals are able to see themselves as objects. This uniqueness makes possible the linking of individuals and society through social processes such as listening, observing, questioning, reading, analyzing, and writing. Discovering yourself promotes critical thinking. For example, to be reflective about who you are and how you have been socialized can help you question your own beliefs and values. Do you hold some stereotypes? Do you value competition over cooperation? To practice sociology in the community, it is important to discover who you are and how you have been shaped by culture.

YOUR ROLE

There are several ways to explore the issue of personal history and its complex relationships with community work and practicing sociology. Your **biography** or **history,** those experiences, beliefs, values, and norms with which you begin your learning outside the classroom, shape the way you listen, observe, question, read, analyze, and write. You need to reflect upon these as you begin any program, trying as best you can to know yourself. Your sense of self has been formed by your past, including your socialization by your parents, school, religion, media, work, and so on. Practicing sociology in the community is also going to shape who you are, making your status and role as an active participant in the community a significant aspect of your educational experience. The people you interact with in the community will shape your sense of self, an ongoing process throughout your life.

We assume that when you are practicing sociology in the community you will also experience many feelings and emotions. If you are participating in a service-learning advocacy program, some of you may experience things in the community that make you emotionally uncomfortable. Teri Karis, in a paper entitled "Pedagogical Approaches to Race and Inequality: Strategies for Addressing Emotional Obstacles" (abstract on-line), suggests some strategies for dealing with "threatening emotions." These include

recognizing feelings such as guilt and helplessness, without getting stuck in them; moving beyond dichotomous thinking to awareness that one can be a 'good person' and have prejudiced thoughts; exploring what to do with one's white privilege [or other's white privilege]; and learning how to translate good intentions into effective action in the world. (2002)

It is also very useful to record these emotions and strategies to deal with them in your journal. Remember that you place filters on your emotions and feelings in much the same ways that you do your listening skills.

Roles are those sets of ideas about what is expected based on the positions you occupy in social relationships. Your status in a community-based learning program brings with it roles that you learn to play. Erving Goffman in *The Presentation of Self in Everyday Life* (1959) provides his readers with a framework for understanding the social interaction process through the device of dramaturgy. According to

Goffman, people are like actors who play roles. They have scripts (culture) and props that they use as they perform in front of an audience.

Like actors, you create impressions of who you are. Goffman referred to this process as "impression management." You carry out this presentation as part of systems that you participate in. For example:

- Define your role in the community or organization.
- What are your ideas about the expectations of the members regarding your role in a community or organization?
- How does your role as a participant in a community-based learning program interact with your gender role?

For those of you who are advocates for social justice, do you experience role conflict with your statuses as student and as an advocate for social change? Immediately you should see the complexity of roles and expectations. Practicing sociology in the community places you in cultures outside the classroom; not only should it help you understand your course material better, but it should also help you to see your own life experiences in a broader context. Broadening your perspective about social life is an important component of practicing sociology in the community.

DIVERSITY

As you begin your community-based learning program, you are likely to be exposed to differences among people. Being exposed to diversity and learning about people who are different from yourself should be a positive benefit of community-based learning (Marullo 1999). You may be in a position to analyze how groups with limited resources and different cultural practices, or ways of life, organize to change their working conditions or inequalities that arise out of diversity.

Observe your community-based field site for the following features of diversity:

Ethnic Relations

How are conflicts handled in the community or organization? Are there differences in outcomes based on ethnicity?

Race Relations

Do people enter into social relationships with others regardless of their race?

Gender Relations

Are women found in positions of power in the organization or community?

Age Group Relations

Is there any apparent age discrimination in the organization or community?

Sexual Orientation Relations

Does everyone have equal access to all benefits in the organization or community? Are gay and lesbian unions recognized in order for them to receive family health benefits?

Able-Bodiedness Relations

Are there opportunities and resources for everyone to move up in the organization? Do people with disabilities have access to technologies that can accommodate personal requirements?

The importance of diversity is found not only in having people with differences in an organization or community. Sociologically and practically, what is important is that all people, regardless of their differences, have a myriad of options available to them as well as the power to make choices among these options.

Diversity is more than a descriptive concept; it also embodies relationships. Write down the previously listed features of diversity in your journal. Add to this list if necessary. Where you are doing your community-based learning program will determine the degree to which you can observe various relationships. We have provided some questions to help you focus your thinking on diversity. These are only examples and you may have different experiences and observations, thus different questions to ask. Take notes on the relationships you observe. Where you surprised by any of your observations? Did any of your observations make you feel uncomfortable? After completing the diversity exercise at the end of this chapter in "Reflections," ask yourself if your history and biography shaped your actions, thinking, or feelings on diversity in your organization or community. Write these ideas down and share them in class, if you feel comfortable doing so.

An awareness of diversity makes practicing sociology a "good fit" with community-based learning programs. Sociologically, we know that individuals are likely to grow up in neighborhoods with people of similar backgrounds, including race and class. These experiences do not necessarily change when you attend college. A walk through the cafeteria provides a segregated view of campus life with groups sitting together because of their common ethnicity.

Based on our teaching experiences, we frequently hear students state their concerns about going into the community and interacting with people unlike themselves (e.g., some students may take an ethnocentric view of these differences). In such instances, the meaning of differences is reinterpreted to mean inferior or unequal. For example, the manner in which people speak, the way they dress, or the color of their skin are differences that are sometimes used to discriminate against some groups. It is important for you to identify your own biases and any ethnocentric views that you hold. Again, this takes critical thinking and reflection.

When you begin your community-based learning program, hopefully you will enter into relationships with new people. Sociologists reason that people's interactions and understanding of the social world are shaped by their own personal and cultural characteristics or, as Mills (1959) states, their biography. If you can identify and understand yourself in relation to diversity, you are more likely to have successful interactions with others in the field and take into account their differences.

Learning about and experiencing diversity is one of the benefits and challenges of participating in a community-based learning program. Practicing critical thinking and critical reflection should help you learn more about yourself as well as learning about others who may share differences. Such an understanding can prepare you for questioning the status quo where the beliefs and values of some groups cannot be realized because of various structural conditions. Learning about diversity and its consequences is excellent preparation for those of you who are interested in practicing sociology in the community in pursuit of social justice.

STEREOTYPES

Stereotypes refer to simplified and often inaccurate generalizations about a group of people. Once categorized, stereotypes make it easy for people to treat members of a group according to these expectations. Stereotypes often lead to inequality and exploitation because they preserve the existing class, race, and gender systems in a society. For example: Homeless people are often stereotyped as lazy, dirty, and illiterate; young black males are stereotyped as dangerous, drug addicts, and less intelligent than young white men; and women are stereotyped as emotional, sex objects, and noncompetitive. The stereotype that the homeless are lazy helps to legitimate a welfare system that focuses on individual characteristics rather than structural arrangements that create and sustain poverty in this society. The stereotype that African-American men are dangerous helps to justify the criminal justice system in the United States that continues to incarcerate young black men at an alarming rate (Bureau of Justice Statistics and The Sentencing Project 2001).

Stereotypes do change over time with changes in the structure of a society. For example, the media today is less apt to depict all women as "housekeepers" as it had in the past. Even so, women are still stereotyped as "caregivers," which helps to preserve the legitimacy of existing gender relations that makes women primarily responsible for caring for their children and their spouses, as well as caring for elderly parents.

Why is stereotyping of interest when practicing sociology in the community? Community-based learning programs can provide the opportunity for "challenging stereotypes" (Hondagneu-Sotelo and Raskoff 1994). You can use your critical thinking to question the status quo. Why are things the way they are? Who benefits? Who does not? In addition to challenging stereotypes in the community, it is also important to expose your own stereotypes. Here are a few steps that may help you do this:

1. Do an inventory of how you think and feel about certain groups. Sometimes listing adjectives is a good way to begin. For example, listing words like lazy, bright, dangerous, and so on.
2. Reflect upon these beliefs. Why do you hold them? How are these assumptions about social groups reinforced?

This process can be done alone, but we suggest it is best accomplished in the classroom. Many people agree that learning sociology is one means of exposing one's own stereotypes as well as those held by other groups. You may be fearful about sharing your biases in the classroom. This is a common feeling among students and you need to move beyond the thinking that if you stereotype you are not a "good person." Once identifying your own stereotypes, doing a community-based learning program often provides you with the opportunity to work with diverse people. Gaining knowledge of other people can help in breaking down stereotypes.

While community-based learning programs can give you the opportunity to gain greater awareness of diversity, they can also reinforce stereotypes (Hamner 2002; Strand 1999). This is so because in community-based learning programs, "students' experience with diverse people not only is fleeting but may also be distorted by the power and prestige inequalities build into the helper-helpee roles" (Strand 1999, 33). Moreover, being exposed to diversity does not necessarily mean that you will be more tolerant or understanding of differences among people. Students in community-based learning programs can also add to stereotyping if they "blame the victim" for his or her problem rather than focusing on structural issues that create and sustain social problems (Hamner 2002). It is important that you challenge your own stereotypes as well as challenging stereotypes that exist in a community or organization.

CONCLUSION

Structure and culture are key concepts in practicing sociology and serve as important links bridging academic sociology and learning in the community. In this chapter, we have asked you to be reflective at your field site. Reflect on how culture shapes relationships and, concurrently, how your own history and biography shape your community experience. Seeing the community through a sociological lens gives you another way to explore your personal future as well as attending to the future of society and, for some, being advocates for social justice.

REFLECTIONS

I. KNOW YOURSELF IN RELATIONSHIP TO DIVERSITY

Doing the following exercise, can help you develop critical thinking, uncover your own biases and assumptions, explore how these biases shape your interactions with others, and practice reflection. When you begin your community-based learning program, you will enter into relationships with new people and groups in the field. If you can identify and understand yourself in relation to diversity, you are more likely to be open to differences among groups. This reflective exercise helps to make explicit your own **biases.** Using the sociological imagination, which embodies critical reasoning, requires that you be aware of these biases. We should note that having these biases is unavoidable. We all have points of view, and we all are selective in what we notice. It would be overwhelming or impossible not to. Share the findings of this exercise with others.

Here is a list of characteristics (adapted from Baird 1996, 81–82) that can help you identify your own personal biases. What is your gender, age, personal appearance, nationality and cultural background, religion, education, physical health, and sexual orientation? Address these same characteristics of your parents. How have these characteristics (and any other characteristics) shaped your experiences and how you understand yourself and relate to others?

II. PROBLEMS WITH LEARNING OUTSIDE THE CLASSROOM

There are at least three potential problems when students work in the community. Review these problems and write a paragraph on whether or not you have experienced any of them. If so, what have you done to address these issues? Share your strategies with others.

1. First, unless properly trained, students engaged in service-learning may fall into the trap of blaming the victim.
2. Second, we have noticed that many students have a difficult time identifying with others unlike them. Some students cannot imagine that they might have the same life chances or possibilities as those less fortunate.
3. Third, students' conceptions of their roles as they enter the community may be problematic. On the one hand, students may see themselves as 'experts' trying to 'fix' the community. On the other hand, students may be paralyzed due to a belief that they do not know enough to have a meaningful effect. (Hironimus-Wendt and Lovell-Troy 1999, 367)

III. OCCUPATIONAL ANALYSIS

When you are practicing sociology in a community or organization, you are exposed to various occupations. We have included this exercise to increase your curiosity about the many occupations in the workplace, to improve your knowledge-gathering techniques using many sources, to stimulate your reflection on how to select an occupation based on facts, and to encourage you to compare various occupations before selecting one.

This exercise has three parts. First, select two occupations in your organization or in the community. Go to the library and locate these occupations in the *Dictionary of Occupational Titles* or any other specialty handbook on occupations. Other sources may include the Internet, face-to-face interviews with persons in this occupation, or telephone interviews with representatives from professional associations such as the American Sociological Association, the American Medical Association.

Next, collect the following information on each occupation and write a two-page description of each occupation:

1. Education and training requirements
2. Entry into the occupation—open or restricted (e.g., medicine)
3. How many people in this occupation?
4. How is the occupation regulated, if it is guild, professional association, or union?
5. Where are these occupations usually employed—types of organizations such as profit, nonprofit, government, and so on?
6. Salary ranges

Finally, address the following questions:

1. What are the major variations between these two occupations?
2. Why are you likely to find these variations?
3. How do you make sense of these?
4. Would you enjoy working in either of these occupations? Explain your answer.

CHAPTER 4

Recording and Reflecting

In this chapter, you will learn new ways of recording and reflecting while working in a community-based learning program. Similar to learning in the classroom, you will need to take notes or make a record of what you hear, see, and read. You will be recording your observations from the field into your personal journal as field notes. You will find when recording in your journal that you will be building upon many of the following: listening, questioning, observing, analyzing, reading, and writing. For example, you will learn to how to make connections between the observations you make in the field and the tentative explanations you are developing. The next step is to link these connections to broader social forces.

In addition to recording these observations, you will be writing memos on the reflections you make about your experiences and the observed patterns of relationships in the field. These patterns will generate ideas and discussion questions you may want to explore in order to find tentative answers or explanations. Thus, your journal is an integral tool to maximize your learning opportunities while working in the community.

Recording in your journal is an informal process, quite different from writing formal papers that are more precise, accurate, and free of emotional content. It is your unique piece of craftsmanship, to be protected carefully. *Remember, recording and reflecting in your journal is a most significant step in doing field research.*

WHAT IS A JOURNAL?

There are many definitions and explanations for what a journal is and what it should include. We share only a few with you. The term journal is inexact and may have different meanings. Some practitioners may describe journals as personal remembrances, reflections on classroom experiences, reaction entries, learning logs, dialectical notebooks, team journals, and anything else collected in notebooks. "Writing is a natural vehicle for exploring ideas, taking them apart, and then reforming them—the essence of thinking. . . . Creating authentic structures for exploratory writing is one of the best ways in which teachers can help their students learn" (Reinertsen and Wells 1993, 182).

An anthropologist distinguishes between a personal diary and a professional notebook when writing field notes. This distinction is useful when learning to write field notes.

> A *personal diary* is a record of what happens to you in everyday life. It tends toward the intimate and it is generally not intended for public consumption. . . . The value of a personal diary is that it often contains information about your deepest, most private, experiences, as well as same-day (or same week) analyses of the meanings of these events in your overall life.
>
> A *professional notebook* is a record of what you observe, hear, overhear, think about, wonder about, and worry about that connects your personal life to your professional one. A common entry might include a statement about something you've read and its application to an event or episode you've observed or lived through in everyday life. (Goodall 2000, 87–88)

We think you will find the distinction between personal diary and professional notebook to be useful when you are learning to write and record field notes. We use the term **journal** in this guide, which we consider the same as a professional notebook. The term *journal* is more familiar language for undergraduate sociology students than *professional notebook*.

We draw from Theodore Wagenaar for our definition of journal. The distinctive feature of this definition is his attention to a sociological perspective.

> It [a journal] is an intellectual exercise in reflexively describing and explaining one's own experiences and observations in terms of a sociological perspective. (1984, 421)

We share with you a journal entry written by a student who planned to study crime victims in a courtroom.

> *I observed again today. The most interesting thing I saw today was a case involving a petitioner who had something wrong with her emotionally/mentally. She was "slow," I guess you could say. She was loud and inappropriate at times, but everyone in the courtroom was very patient and kind to her. I was happy to see that. If anyone else had acted the way she did, I'm sure they would've been seriously reprimanded. I felt really bad for the petitioner because she was claiming that her ex-boyfriend tried to get her into prostitution and wanted to be her pimp. I definitely believed her when she claimed that and I felt so bad for her that she was almost taken advantage of by the respondent. Luckily she knew that she didn't want to be a prostitute and was able to tell her mother and the police about it in order to stop him from dragging her into prostitution. The judge ruled in her favor and*

she expressed so much happiness. It made me feel like I witnessed justice being served. I left the courtroom feeling really good about the court system, which I rarely feel.

Reflect on how you might explain these observations drawing from a sociological perspective. We suggest you review Chapters 2 and 3 for ideas and concepts to use in your explanations.

In your journal you will be recording observations on the kinds of social relationships that you observe and engage in while participating in your learning environment. Your observations become your field notes and your data. Your reflections on these data become part of your interpretations. *Remember, no two journals will be alike, in part, because your observations and recording of observations are shaped by your own history and current experiences in the field.*

WHAT TO RECORD

A primary purpose of a community-based learning program is to integrate classroom learning with the knowledge you gain from the community or workplace. This requires that you record detailed, descriptive field notes about the people and activities that you observe in the community. In this section, we provide you with ideas on what to record in your journal. Quite often your faculty advisor will provide you with instructions, but that is not always the case, especially in less structured courses. You must choose what fits best with your learning style and the course requirements, which are usually stated on your course syllabus. If you are unsure about how to proceed, please consult the professor teaching the course. There is no right or wrong way to organize your journal.

When you arrive at your organization or community, write down your first impressions of the place and the people immediately after you leave the field. Often it is useful to take a trip to the bathroom to jot down notes in a small spiral notebook that you carry in your pocket or purse. *You will only have first impressions once,* and these will disappear quickly as you meet more people and interact more often. The emotions you feel as you experience your first day in the community or organization are of utmost importance to record, and are discussed later in the chapter. You will likely find that these feelings will change as you spend more time in the community or organization. In the sections that follow, we discuss the journal format in more depth.

FIELD NOTES AND OBSERVATIONS

When you write field notes you are writing a continual commentary to yourself about what you are observing and how you are beginning to reflect on these observations. Field notes are idiosyncratic to you. It is crucial that the notes be as detailed as possible and recorded as promptly as possible. When you write a field note you are making a commentary about what is happening in the research, involving both observation and analysis. We argue that you separate these from one another. One way to write useful field notes is to write down whatever impressions happen rather than to sift out what may seem important to you. You may not know until later what will be useful. A key to successful field notes is to keep asking the questions, "what am I learning?" and "how does this case differ from the last" (Huber and VandeVen 1995, 74)?

Sometimes students have difficulty knowing what and how to describe what they have observed. We have found when teaching this course that students often write prescriptive and normative statements, such as ". . . people should be more friendly to me and invite me to lunch" or "everyone is really great in the office." These statements, while reflective of how students feel, may not be useful if these are not accompanied with some descriptions of behavior. For example, what behaviors and actions by the people in the community could lead you to conclude that everyone is really great? You could be misinterpreting their actions. It is very important to record these first impressions and to have them available in your journal for comparative purposes later in the semester. In the text that follows we review suggestions from experienced fieldworkers.

If this is a new experience for you and you don't know where to start, the following ideas on what to describe may be useful. Describe, in detail, the physical aspects of the community or organization. This is often referred to as "mapping" and is often useful data later in the study. Our students found it useful to draw a map on a separate sheet of paper on which they labeled the setting in which they were observing. It helped to refresh their memories when they returned to write their field notes. There are several ways to start recording what you are observing.

There are at least two rules to follow when writing field notes: (1) Be concrete, and (2) distinguish verbatim accounts from those that are paraphrased or based on general recall (Lofland and Lofland 1995, 93). Some argue that you should record everything you observe, while others suggest that you focus on two or three significant events. Here is some general advice:

1. Write down everything in detail.
2. Write about everybody, no matter how insignificant he or she may seem to you.
3. Document conversations verbatim.
4. Pay close attention to stories.
5. Do not censor your field notes. (Silver and Perez 1998, 351)

This is not an exhaustive list.

Another technique for journal writing and recording is the "critical incident technique" (Stanton and Ali 1994). This is a useful technique and can be enjoyable to write. Also, it ties directly into work on objectives. You should sit down at least once a week, choose one or two critical incidents, and explore them in detail in your journal. Here are some suggestions for organizing your reflections and writing.

1. Identify the event or occurrence with as much specificity as possible.
2. Describe the relevant details surrounding the event: what, when, how, why, where.
3. List the people involved and their relationships to everyone.
4. Describe your role, your actions, and so on.
5. Analyze the incident. How did you handle it? Would you do the same thing the next time? Why or why not?
6. Analyze this incident in terms of its impact on you. Discuss why it is a critical incident. Where do you go from here? (Stanton and Ali 1994, 67–68)

REFLECTIONS

Sometimes students do not benefit from the journal process because they are unclear about what to record in the journal. One real value of the journal is to use this as a place to record your reflections on your experiences. You might want to focus on two or three main ideas of concern and write about these in detail. Be cautious, because the key to a successful journal is to be as ". . . open and honest as you can about what you have thought, felt, or did and what your impressions are after you have time to reflect" (Baird 1996, 15). On the other hand, remember to protect your journal from others who should not read it or could cause you harm if they read it. To ensure their protection, some researchers prefer to keep their field notes and reflections on their computer.

Like others who have taught service-learning and community-based learning, we encourage you to engage in critical reflection (Hollis 2002). By this we mean, you learn by reflecting on your observations and experiences in the community and connecting these with sociological concepts and principles. While doing this, you are examining your own personal beliefs and how these may shape your observations and interpretations. The rigor you use in recording in your journal is significant to your success in critical reflection.

We share with you a journal entry from the same student studying victims in the courtroom. She records her observations, and describes her feelings in the bracketed material at the end of the entry:

> *Today was my last day of observation. I thought that court would already be in session when I arrived at the courtroom, since I was running late, but luckily it wasn't. People were getting annoyed that it was taking so long to start. Once it was finally in session, court went pretty much the same as usual. There were a lot of dismissed cases due to the absence of the petitioner (and sometimes even the respondent), all of the CPOs were approved by the judge, and so on. [I wanted to stay until 1 P.M. but by 12:15 P.M. all of the respondents and petitioners had left the room, and I was the only person left sitting in the audience. One of the lawyers looked over at me and so did the judge. I felt weird and didn't want them to ask me any questions, so I just got up and left. I'm glad I did because the most interesting part of my day was when I left the courtroom and eavesdropped on a conversation that three domestic violence advocates were having, one of whom was a young woman I met during one of my previous days of observing. One of them was saying how frustrated she is that she's not making a difference in the system like she originally thought she could. Another one of the women disagreed and said that she felt she really is making a difference. Then the conversation shifted to feminism and I lost interest in what they were saying, so I decided I would just leave for the day. I really hope I put in enough time for observing.]*

This student had finished her observations for this project and had learned that not all her data would be generated in the actual courtroom. People who are engaged in courtroom activities also frequently meet in the environs outside the courtroom. This might prove to be an important source of data in future study in terms of social interactions and potential relationships pertinent to her project.

IMPRESSIONS AND EMOTIONS

We assume that when you are learning in the community you will experience and express subjective feelings and emotions. We further assume that your emotions and feelings will influence your observations, your journal entries, and ultimately your reflections and analysis. Lastly, we assume that you need to recognize the constant interplay between the personal, the emotional, and the intellectual work you will engage in during your time in the community or an organization. For example, you may struggle with your emotional responses if those you study are so different from you that you cannot begin to understand them (Gilbert 2001). Review the discussion of emotional labor in Chapter 3.

For these and many other reasons, we encourage you to record your emotional reactions during your research, separate from field notes and other information. Sherryl Kleinman and Martha Copp (1993, 52) argue that when you read fieldwork accounts, in this case your journal entries, you should ask "How did the researcher's emotions play a part in the data collection and analysis of this group or setting?" In most classes, students are trained to deny any emotions toward participants. So, frequently students do not reflect on how they feel, for example, on why they feel pleased when others like them, or displeased when people do not like them. If you carefully record your feelings in your journal separate from your observations, it will help you to recognize if you are being biased in your interpretations of the data.

Our experience with students has been that they spoke frequently about, and wrote in their journals, that they were pleased to be able to acknowledge their emotions in a university classroom and workplace assignment. Their educational experience and training, to date, had precluded this opportunity. They began to search for an understanding of how these emotions might influence what they saw, what they recorded, and how they analyzed their observations.

There are many opportunities for you to experience different emotions during your field experience. These need to be recorded in your journal starting at the very first contact you have with people in the field. We discuss these opportunities in terms of several processes associated with fieldwork (Berg 2001, 136–139, 171–173).

1. The entry process: getting in
2. The initiation process: getting acquainted
3. Prolonged engagement process: getting accepted
4. The disengagement process: getting out

The Entry Process: Getting In

We require our students to begin recording in their journal before starting fieldwork. Thus, the beginning entries include the process you used to obtain approval to participate in a community-based learning program. There are likely to be many emotions associated with "getting in" to an organization or gaining access to work in a community. Students often express in class and in their journals how "nervous" they were trying to locate a place to do their community-based learning for the semester. In fact, some students even expressed terror about approaching strangers to make appointments for an interview. Some were uncomfortable with the uncertainty of getting in, and some expressed their fear of being rejected or refused entry.

The following example shows how the same student made entries in her journal as she made several attempts to study victims of crime in a courthouse. The end of her entry shows some of her reflections based on her observations.

> *During my time observing I wasn't really able to observe what I needed, which were victims of crime. There were some but not a lot. I didn't realize it would be so difficult to find victims in a courtroom. I need to find out more about courthouses in general, and hopefully about this specific courthouse, that way next time I don't feel so lost. There are not many clients with lawyers (i.e., there are not many victims to observe).*
>
> *[Should I maybe alter my project? For example, should I make it criminal cases that I observe instead of civil? Should I pick a certain crime? If so, it should be crime where the victims go the court often].*

This student records the potential problems she faces to complete her project because of a lack of clients in the courtroom. Her reflections on her observations suggest a possible need to adjust her project directions.

You are encouraged to select an organization or community that corresponds to your own interests and capabilities. The process is made easier if you start where you are so that you begin with your interests and questions (Lofland and Lofland 1995). Students who selected social service organizations often commented at the beginning and end of their course that they wanted to find out if social service work "was for them." Some students commented that their learning experiences in a women's shelter or with abused children helped them to decide their career and future education goals. Other students commented that their internship experience changed their career directions so that they did not go to graduate school in a particular field.

The descriptions that students wrote in their journals about the search process for a community-based learning site were frequently referred to during the semester. Students often expressed emotions of triumph, joy, and pleasure as they reread their previous entries of terror, fright, and uncertainty. This suggests that their emotions, hopes, and fears, did influence their perceptions of their experiences in learning in their community-based learning program.

The Initiation Process: Getting Acquainted

Some of the same emotions that you will experience with getting into an organization are expressed with "getting acquainted." Once you have gained access, there is further concern about "fitting in" with peers and being liked. Several students wrote in their journals that they felt "left out" if they were not included in a lunch engagement when others were. They often commented on who ate with whom and who was included in other social functions. Being excluded left them feeling like "outsiders" and being rejected. Students expressed in their journals many times that it was very important for them to feel comfortable with their peers in the organization. Unless they felt comfortable, the students noted they were reluctant to ask people for information or assistance. When you include these emotions and feelings in your journal, faculty can make suggestions on how to correct the situation to enhance your learning experiences, especially when these are shared in the classroom.

Prolonged Engagement Process: Getting Accepted

Our students typically spend twelve or more hours a week for a semester in their organization or community. Schools on a quarter or other system may have fewer opportunities. Thus, the engagement experience will be briefer, although not necessarily less intense. You will have many opportunities to persistently observe patterns and relationships and to interact with the same people. Consequently, you may find that you become emotionally attached to some of your associates. Some of our students noted in their journals that they really liked the people with whom they worked. This is especially the case for students who worked in social service agencies such as halfway houses, women's shelters, or agencies established to protect women and children. Other students have indicated a strong dislike for their coworkers. They asked to share these in class to explore ways to cope with these feelings. Other students may not feel as connected to their peers as they would like.

The Disengagement Process: Getting Out

Often our students wrote in their journals and expressed in class that they were sad to leave the community, especially in a social service environment. For example, one group of students working with educationally and behaviorally challenged children chose not to leave. They continued their role as interns during the summer and another semester, even though they received no academic credit or payment for their efforts. They felt, to some extent, as though they were deserting these people when the internship period ended.

Here are some closing tips when leaving your community or organization:

1. Be sure they know in advance when and why you are leaving.
2. Bring closure to your other working relationships.
3. Organize your projects in such a way that someone else can continue them.
4. Be sure to communicate the appreciation you feel to everyone for the care and time they gave you during your internship. (Stanton and Ali 1994, 53)

These tips can be used in all community-based learning programs.

You need to write a final entry in the journal in which you focus on evaluation. For example, you might address such questions as the following:

1. Did you meet your learning objectives? Explain how. (This assumes that you developed learning objectives early in your community-based learning program. These should be part of an appendix in your journal so that you can return to these at the end of the field work.)
2. What was your most important contribution? (Did you feel you made a contribution? This assumes you chose a field work site where you could make some meaningful contribution.)
3. In what ways did your internship disappoint you? (Another way to get at the same idea would be to think about how you could improve your experience in a community-based learning program.)
4. What new skills did you develop or hone? (It is important that you answer this question in some depth and reflect on the new skills you have developed. These should be kept as a separate section of your journal.)
5. How did your relationship with your supervisor either help or hinder you in meeting your goals? (This may be a difficult question to answer because at times you may have no supervisor or it may not be clear who your supervisor is. In some situations you may have more than one supervisor. Your reflections on this question will be useful to you when you leave the field and go on to other experiences.)
6. What were the highlights of your internship?
7. List tips for future interns who select this site. (Green 1997, 152–153)

Even though Marianne Green is addressing internships, doing this evaluation would be useful to you in all community-based learning programs. Also, answers to these questions will be very useful to you if you are going to look for a job or apply to a graduate program. For example, you may identify some workers who were especially pleased with your contribution and ask them for a letter of recommendation. These facts will be useful to you in writing a resume. *Be sure to get permission to use someone's name as a reference on your resume.*

ACTIVITIES

As mentioned earlier, the journal can serve as a record of the number and types of skills you acquired during your community-based learning program. Establish a service record in the back of your journal in which you keep a running total of the number of hours spent in different activities, such as taking notes at a meeting, writing up the minutes of the meeting that become an official record, processing data, literature searches, answering the phone and making appointments, writing reports, and many other activities. The data from this service record can be very useful to you when you apply for a job at a later time. It provides a record of your specific skills and tells your future employer how capable you are. When you are recording your activities, try to imagine how they will be useful to you later. Listed below is an example of how you might organize your activities chart at the beginning of the semester. You will probably enlarge and reorganize this chart to include in your portfolio for when you apply for employment after graduation.

General Administrative Work: Preparing and sending newsletters, putting together information packets, writing quick memos or letters, buying office supplies, setting up and organizing files

General Information: Filing systems, scanning for information, mailings, inquiries, e-mail, computer access, telephones

Press Conference: Notifying others via e-mail and fax, preparing memos and press releases, contacting officials for information, working with the media to organize participants and their programs

All of these skills are transferable to other organizations, as well as to working as an advocate for some community project. When you are recording your activities, try to imagine how these will be useful to you later.

BACKGROUND INFORMATION

An important component of critical thinking skills is reading, as discussed in the previous chapter. What you read and how you select these readings are important for developing the ability to ask and answer critical questions that will help you with the important task of understanding how and why organizations or communities function as they do.

We suggest that you keep in this section any documents you collect that may have important information for you to know or have available for reference later or for analysis. Some of you will be doing your community-based learning program in a large organizational setting. This provides an excellent opportunity to learn firsthand how people interact and develop relationships in organizations and communities. To learn this, you need to review some of the following information at some time during your fieldwork. However, some of this information can be gathered before and during your initial interview with the organization.

1. What is the mission of the organization?
2. What are the goals and structure of the organization?
3. What is the organizational culture?
4. What are the major products of the organization?

Some of this background information can be stored in your journal so that it is in one place and thus available to you when you are reflecting on your observations and doing your analysis.

For illustration purposes, we review the first question and some of our students' experiences with finding answers to the question on the organization's mission. One of the authors who taught this course found that students were often hesitant and uncomfortable asking for such information. One way they approached this was to go on the Internet and look for information and answers. Others said they did not like the language of *mission* so they revised the question in a way that was more comfortable for them. For example, instead of asking what is the mission, they asked what is your main purpose. After they had became more familiar with the organization, they would ask for a mission statement. Most students were amazed to learn that most workers did not know what a mission statement was and had never seen one. They were even more surprised to learn that some people had received one but put it away and never looked at it again. We encouraged the students to look for other documents in the organization that might give them answers.

We used this as a teaching moment and had students explore the mission of their own college by asking the department, the dean, the vice president, and others for a copy of their mission. This was actually an enlightening experience for everyone since many places in the organization had no record of such documents, nor were they aware of such in the entire university. We then asked the students to reflect in their journals on what it means if the organization does not have a written statement of why it is in existence. Several explanations were offered by the students: "Everyone knows what a university is supposed to be doing so there is no need for a mission statement." "It is clear to me, professors teach and students learn. What more do you need to know?" Another possible explanation is that the students did not make clear what they needed from the persons with whom they spoke. Or the people were too busy in everyday activities and survival to be very concerned with having a formal mission statement. One student said people in the administration were surprised that such a request would be made and perhaps the professor teaching the course was new to the university. This explanation did not hold up since the professor had taught there for over thirty years.

Another series of questions may be a useful guide to help you organize your first impression of an organization. You do not need to answer all of these, but they provide you a place to begin. Write down your answers to these questions to clarify your own thinking. To do this, you need to reflect upon your observations.

1. What does your organization look like? Your office (if you have one)?
2. How do you feel when you are there?
3. How long has your organization and your section been in existence?
4. What do these people do? How do they dress? Act? Talk?
5. Who are the clients/customers of your organization? Are they visible, what do they look like? What do they act like? (Stanton and Ali 1994, 70)

The first question, what does your organization look like, can be interpreted several ways. For example, what is the structure of the organization in terms of positions, occupations, communication channels, and many other features of organization structure? In our community-based learning program, students were advised to ask for a current organization chart so that they could learn how to communicate and with whom, and what were the main positions of authority. Again, the students were surprised to learn that in their placement organization, people did not have an organization chart or were unwilling to share it. Students explored the meaning of these findings and wondered if keeping such information was a means of controlling how information was passed on in the organization. On the other hand, most people knew who their bosses were and that seemed to satisfy them, according to the students. Obviously, these are superficial explanations and if one were doing research or advocacy work, much more information would need to be acquired.

In addition to documents from your community or organization, we suggest you include in this section "reading summaries" that draw from your own discoveries from what you read. We encourage you to write a one or two-page summary of articles or books that you think are related to your work. Also, we suggest you write a brief paragraph on why you selected the reading, if it met your purpose, and if it stimulated other thoughts and readings.

MEMOS

Mills reminds us in *The Sociological Imagination* (1959) that we need to be writing about our research constantly, not just when we finish it or want to get money for a research project. One useful form of writing is analytic memos. "Memos are primarily conceptual in nature. They don't report data; they tie together different pieces of data into a recognizable cluster, often to show that those data are instances of a general concept" (Miles and Huberman 1994, 72). Memos are a tool for reflecting on what you are doing throughout your community-based learning program. You may write memos as certain relationships appear in your coded data and you have some tentative thoughts on this relationship that you want to reflect on. Critical reflection keeps you actively engaged in your community-based learning program.

When you are doing your journal work and writing memos, new ideas and challenging questions will emerge that you will want to find answers to. "Memos do for ideas what field notes and transcripts do for perception: They convert thought into form that allows examination and further manipulation" (Maxwell 1996, 12). Reflection and analysis go hand in hand.

In this chapter, we provide you with some ideas and guidance, not fixed rules and procedures. You need to record what will be useful to you in meeting your learning goals and objectives. In addition to recording your observations about what you have learned, we want you to reflect on these observations and to raise questions about them. Next, we want you to analyze these observations so that you move beyond the relationships within the organization and community.

In summary, what you record in your journal is very important. It is your data base for analysis and comparison. It links your journal to your coursework and it bridges the university and community. It provides an excellent record of your progress during the semester and helps you learn how you have adapted during various phases or stages of your program. The journal provides specific information on the types of duties and assignments you have completed and feel competent to perform again, often in later employment. It is also a tool for reflecting on the factors that influenced you more in one direction or another relative to your career and education goals. It provides a basis for developing trust with another adult person, your faculty advisor. *Remember, record your field notes on the same day you are in the field and include as much detail as possible. Describe your reflections in detail and transcribe them promptly.*

HOW TO RECORD

An important part of your activity in your community-based learning program will be learning to take field notes. They may take several forms: mental notes, jotted notes, and complete field notes. Mental notes are often the first notes you will make, and these usually consist of trying to remember items like who and how many individuals were present, the physical environment, who spoke to whom and about what, what type of movement took place as individuals interacted, and a general chronology of events (Lofland and Lofland 1995). Many students find the major organizing principle for keeping their notes is chronology because it aids their recall and reflections if they recreate each day in the evening when they are done. It also helps to establish a disciplined approach early in the field.

The process of recording in a small notebook will help you direct your mind at a later time to recall events when you have time to write these, hopefully at the end of the day. Jotted notes are useful when you sit down to write your completed notes. It is important that you remember that jotted notes are not field notes. You need to transcribe these jotted notes at the end of the day you record them or sooner, if possible. *Be sure you put a date on these recordings for future reference.*

Here is an example of jotted notes and how you might turn these into complete field notes:

Day 1: Nervous; want to give good impression; fun children
Day 2: Nervous; no one to help me; don't know what to do
Day 3: Told to help out, which means ???
Day 4: Nervous; don't feel useful
Day 5: Children great to work with

The next step for you would be to take these jotted notes and write full statements from them. For example, describe in depth how you felt when you were not useful. What specific *behavior* were you engaged in that made you feel useless? Describe what others around you were doing and your interactions with them that left you feeling useless. Describe how the leaders informed you, if they did, about what you should be doing with the children so that you could be useful. Describe your "nervous" behavior in terms of your interactions with the children and others. After reading your completed notes, reflect on how you might gain a better understanding of what you are missing and how to improve your contribution and reduce your nervousness.

Make your entries in a spiral notebook, using only one side of the page (Wagenaar 1984, 431). With this procedure, faculty can make comments on the facing page. This makes the writing easier to read. Two approaches can be used regarding the style of the entry. In one, the description of the event or behavior is separated from the analysis. This approach encourages a clear separation between description and analysis. In the other approach, the description and analysis are combined.

In order to use the information for analytic purposes, you need to be concrete when writing your field notes. For example, if you record that someone was nice, that may be of little use to you when comparing that with others' behavior. A concrete note might include the following: The person (using pseudo names) sought me out and invited me to attend an important meeting from which I would have been excluded if the person had not found me. Be specific.

After you have been recording for a while, you will begin to formulate ideas that are not part of your observations. You might want to put these into your field notes or write them as a memo, regardless of how trivial you think these may be. Our students found it useful to put these thoughts in parentheses in the journal. This procedure is useful for when you do your analysis because you can quickly identify your ideas and possible inferences from your data, your observations.

The use of the computer makes it easier to duplicate samples of your journal entries to use in classroom discussion and analysis. It provides space on the back of pages where faculty can write their comments. Also, the computer increases the privacy and confidentiality of your journal because you have the only access to the data entries. Thus, privacy, security, and simplicity of duplicating are important advantages of using a computer to log your entries. Whatever method you select, use one that compliments your usual way of doing your work. *Remember, carry a small spiral notebook to record brief, jotted notes when you are in the field.*

WHERE TO RECORD

Where you do your recording is also very important. Unless you have asked for permission to interview someone and to take notes, do not assume that it is acceptable to the person being interviewed. *If you want to write openly, ask for permission.* This can be done in an easy manner by saying "Do you mind if I make some notes while you are talking?" Be prepared to answer questions about what you plan to do with these notes.

In oral cultures, watching and writing about people may seem strange behavior to those living there (Emerson, Fretz and Shaw 1995, 25). Do not write your notes on the behavior while you are observing it because people may think you are writing about them. You may risk offending others when the focus of the jotting appears to be the current activity or topics. Jot your notes down inconspicuously so that you do not raise the anxieties of the people you are observing by openly writing down everything you see or hear.

To this point, we have focused on what you need to do to create a useful journal for your later analysis and for your assignments. We mentioned earlier in the chapter that the journal provides a mechanism for you to communicate with faculty who direct the course. That is why we have spent so much time trying to convince you of the meaningfulness of your journal. You should expect your faculty director to give you feedback that will help you to produce a meaningful and complete journal. Because faculty are providing challenging feedback to you, we ask you to read the feedback, sign your initials, and add more comments as applicable. We have found that some students do not read the faculty comments and feedback if they think the journal is not being graded. *Remember, keeping a journal is not busy work. It is a helpful and necessary tool for learning in the community. It is an important technique and valuable to you, if you decide to invest your time.*

WHY KEEP A JOURNAL?

Your journal is a primary teaching tool in the process of cultivating the depth dimension associated with critical thinking. Learning is one major purpose of community-based learning programs; one of the major tools for facilitating learning is the process of keeping a journal. Keeping a journal during your program is a demanding process, and it requires discipline. We tend to forget much of what we have observed. Thus, it is essential to record as soon as possible notes that will help you remember what happened.

There are many pedagogical and practical benefits that come from keeping a journal. In fact, students often comment that when they re-read their journal a year or so later, they continue to learn and improve their skills. Listed in the text that follows are some of the benefits we hope you will experience while recording in your journal.

PEDAGOGICAL BENEFITS

A major requirement for learning in a community-based learning program is that it be an intellectual and cognitive experience. Thus, it is crucial that your community-based learning program provide many opportunities for you to bring back to the classroom thorough descriptions of your learning experiences. These become the data for discussion, for your sociological analysis of the patterns you observe, and for reflection. Other pedagogical benefits of keeping a journal include those listed at the top of the next page.

- Assisting you in monitoring your progress in developing observational, critical thinking, and analytic skills in the field
- Serving as a communication vehicle for you and your professor so that problems and issues can be identified early and remedies can be developed
- Collecting field notes for use in a community action project or a research paper
- Reflecting on field site observations and beginning to formulate questions and ideas about connections and patterns you are observing
- Identifying patterns of social relationships within the field site that can be analyzed using sociological concepts
- Redirecting your learning from passive to active voice, which emphasizes the process of inquiry rather than memorization
- Recording notes about questions, ideas, or discussion that you wish to study further
- Preparing you to engage in social change and social advocacy

PRACTICAL BENEFITS

There are many obvious practical reasons for you to participate in a community-based learning program. These are likely to be maximized if you are disciplined and systematic in recording in your journal. Your journal provides you with a chronology of the time you spent in one organization that it would be impossible to remember. It requires that you be systematic, rigorous, and disciplined in order to receive these practical benefits. Some of these benefits include the following:

- Retaining a history of meaningful events and activities in the field site for present and future use
- Identifying ways to cope with tensions in the field by writing and describing the problems, conflicts, issues, and emotions you experience in the field
- Capturing the distinct stages of your adaptation to your organization
- Keeping a chronology of tasks performed and skills developed for use when you write a resume
- Developing contacts so that you are able to obtain letters of recommendation from the persons who supervised you
- Providing you the opportunity to develop and apply skills for social action and advocacy

The above lists are not exhaustive or mutually exclusive. Perhaps by the end of the semester you will be able to add to the benefits you have experienced from keeping your personal journal. *Remember, recording and reflecting in a disciplined, systematic way are two significant components of your learning in a community-based learning program.*

ETHICAL ISSUES

There are many ethical issues you will encounter when doing community-based research. These will not be clearly identified or defined for you. Nor will there be clear statements on what you should do about these. It is primary importance that you show respect to everyone with whom you interact. Second, you should obtain a copy of the *Ethical Standards of the American Sociological Association Sections 1-11.08* (ASA 1997). Your professor will probably have a copy of this or can direct you in obtaining a copy from ASA. Here are some of the topics covered in this publication: competence, representation and misuse of expertise, nondiscrimination, nonexploitation, harassment, conflicts of interest, confidentiality and maintaining confidentiality, limits of confidentiality, anonymity of sources, and minimizing intrusions on privacy. We suggest that you ask your professor for classroom time to discuss this publication and the specific ethical issues you have experienced in your community-based learning program. Our experience with students is that the most lively classroom discussions centered on ethical issues.

We discuss only two of these in this section: privacy and confidentiality. Both issues are interconnected and part of protecting yourself, your university, and the community. Privacy issues are of concern to you and the people you are observing. First of all, until you have built up a relationship of trust between you and your supervisor or faculty member, you may want to confine your entries in your journal to somewhat neutral statements that do not violate your private thoughts and reactions. When there is trust between you and the person reading your journal entries, you may want to confide your major concerns and problems in your journal. This can be a "teachable moment" for the faculty member to use, while maintaining your privacy. However, we are not suggesting that you sanitize your entries. This is a delicate line to walk and there are no hard and fast rules. Finally, to protect your privacy further, you must have a safe place for your journal.

There are ethical issues that may arise while you are doing your observations. For example, some of our students have observed what they considered to be illegal behavior, and have been asked to lie or misrepresent what they considered to be the truth. Students have reported such occurrences in their journals and discussed these in the classroom so that others could learn from their experiences.

You need to protect the privacy of your university and the people with whom you work. For example, when you record your observations, you must be sure to disguise the names of all participants, their identities and specific roles, and the field site to protect the anonymity of the participants. The first day use pseudo names for everyone in the study, including the organization or community in which you are located. It has happened that students have lost their journals and information has become available to persons who should not have had it. If you have not protected the anonymity of the community members, you may cause harm to others. Protecting others extends to talking to people about your research. Do not identify your sources unless you have explicit permission to do so. You have an ethical obligation to leave the field the way you found it, not contaminating it for others. Although you will do all you can to protect people's identities, there may be times when someone will figure out what they said in a written report, in spite of what you have done to protect them. For this and other reasons, it is important to consider ethical issues all during your research project.

Also, it is important to protect community members so they can fully trust you not to violate their confidentiality. This may be difficult to do in some instances, especially when you are engaged in social action and advocacy work. When doing advocacy research, there may be some information that you can share with community members but that information does *not* include your field notes and observations, your reflections on your observations, and your impressions and emotions during your community-based learning experience.

There will be some information that you should share with community members when you are doing advocacy research. For example, if you learn of meetings to be held that will affect the community, you will want to share this information so that people are empowered to participate. Doing advocacy is more than developing sociological knowledge, doing advocacy is applying that knowledge and creating social change. This promotes the idea of sharing rather than protecting community members. We agree with sociologists Sam Marullo and Bob Edwards (2000, 910) who state, "If the service activity is not empowering recipients, it further alienates those in need, separating them from their just place in society."

CONCLUSION

This chapter has introduced you to the value of keeping a journal throughout your community-based learning experience, beginning when you first try to find a placement, to the point of disengaging from the field and completing the course requirements. The journal process usually covers the entire semester. Thus, it is a developmental process during which trust should build between you, your professor, and the community. Even though your experience will be brief, it is necessary for you to be systematic and disciplined in your observations and recordings. The primary purpose in this chapter has been to provide some guidance, but you will make the decisions of structure, content, format, and thoroughness. There is no right or wrong way to organize your work. We encourage you to write in as much detail as possible in your journal, to increase the likelihood that your analysis and writing will be true and plausible. We close this chapter with a quote that illustrates, in poetic fashion, the value of keeping a journal.

> Through journal writing, sociology students have the opportunity to mentally pass through the garden of information they read and hear, the concepts and theories that are explained to them, and their own personal experiences, and to collect a bouquet that unites or links some of these elements. (Reinertsen and DaCruz 1996, 102)

REFLECTIONS

I. JOURNAL ORGANIZATION

We have proposed one way to organize your journal by dividing it into several sections. Be sure to date each entry.

Sample Journal Format and Organization

Section 1: Field Notes and Observations

In this section, record your field notes and observations on your organization or community. Write descriptively in as much detail as possible, so that you get the most data from your fieldwork. Record new words or any new use of words already familiar to you.

Section 2: Reflections

In this section, record the reflections you make about your experiences and the observed patterns of relationships in the field. You may find it useful to put these in brackets when you are writing in the field.

Section 3: Impressions and Emotions

In this section, record personal impressions and emotions that you experience during your fieldwork. It is natural to experience feelings about the work and people you will be working with. However, keep these separate from your observations of what people do.

Section 4: Activities

In this section, record the activities that you engage in, such as answering or making phone calls, writing letters, interviewing community members for their ideas on what problems they are experiencing, organizing community events, and other tasks. Include any skills you use, especially new skills you acquire and old skills you improve on.

Section 5: Background Information

In this section, record background information, for example, any documents you collect from your observation so that you have an up-to-date list to refer to when you write your paper and to include in your appendix. We recommend also that you keep "reading summaries" in this section that draw from your own discoveries. These summaries can be less than one page and should include a paragraph on why you selected this reading and if it gave you what you wanted.

Section 6: Memos

In this section you begin writing memos during the period when you start your community or research project. These memos refer to any writing that you do other than your field notes or coding on your project. Memos are written to facilitate reflection.

We ask you to reflect on this format by reviewing the following questions.

1. How useful to you in your work was this format?
2. Did you alter this format in your fieldwork?
3. Try to think of another way for organizing your journal entries. Explain your choices.
4. Would you include the time you spent in the organization in each observation instead of at the end in a separate section? Why or why not?

II. CRITICAL THINKING AND RECORDING

As part of your recording, include entries on what you are reading during your community-based learning program. This reading may include material on current events, sociological studies, or any other pertinent material. Make these entries a "critical evaluation" of your readings. Make certain you are doing analysis and not just describing what you have read. Look for your own biases and those of others in your evaluation. Ask yourself if the sources of information are valid. Then give yourself reflective space. Think about what you have read from as many perspectives as possible. Be open to new ideas. Question assumptions (adapted from Reinertsen and Wells 1993, 182–186).

III. ORGANIZATION MISSION

This is a practice exercise to prepare you for your placement or community assignment. Two objectives should be accomplished if you do this exercise correctly: (1) You will learn more about your college or university, which is valuable information to empower you; (2) you will learn to take initiative in finding where information can be found in an organization and how to obtain it. First, go to your catalogue and find the organization's structure. Next, go to the Vice President's Office for Academic Affairs or a similar office that would likely know where the organization mission is stated. Obtain a copy of the university mission. Next, go to the dean of the School of Arts and Sciences or the school that you are part of and ask for the mission of that school. Then go to the sociology department and ask for a copy of the department's mission (if they have one).

Compare the mission statements from each source. How are these missions different or similar?

Can you come up with some tentative explanations for these differences or similarities?

If any of these sources do not have a mission statement, interview responsible sources to learn why this is the situation. Reflect on your learning experiences. Put this exercise in your journal for future reference.

CHAPTER 5

Doing Field Research

When you are practicing sociology in a community-based learning program, you will need some basic knowledge of how to do field research. Whether you are doing volunteer work, an internship, service-learning, or a service-learning advocacy program, you need to know how to ask and answer questions and what to do with the answers. Whatever your objective, you need to know how to get information on what is going on in a community or organization. If you do not seek this knowledge, you will not be engaged with what is happening around you, you will have nothing to ask about or write about in your journal, and you will not be active in thinking about social issues and finding the problematic in these issues. You need a context to put your observations into, otherwise there is little opportunity to make sense of your observations.

Your project may well be to explore an idea and to gain tentative answers to the questions you generated. Hopefully, you and the organization or community will be thinking about how you can use these answers to pursue social advocacy. This guide is to share with you a few skills that field and other researchers use to seek answers to questions that arise from their work and from the community in which they are participating. These include participant observation, interviewing, coding and organizing your data, and making sense of your data and theorizing. However, this is not a textbook on research methods. The purpose is to acquaint you with some of the methods that sociologists use to generate and apply knowledge. Possibly you will have some previous knowledge of how to do research and this will be a review for you.

We begin by discussing field research and its variations of studies, followed by planning a community project. Then we discuss in more depth how to do field research. We do not provide a complete review of the many variations and possibilities. If you want further information or to delve into some of the complexities of field research in depth, we suggest you read the references we have used to give you this brief review of doing field research. We conclude with a discussion of how to tell the stories of the community or organization.

WHAT IS FIELD RESEARCH?

There are many types of studies you can do while practicing sociology in a community. These may include, for example, surveys, archival studies, historical studies, case studies, ethnographies, and statistical comparative studies. We refer to these types of studies as research strategies that you use to plan your study. Every study needs to have a clear strategy or set of strategies. These strategies are shaped by (1) the type of research questions you and the community ask, (2) the extent of control you and the community have over actual behavioral events, and (3) the degree of focus on contemporary or historical events in the community (Yin 2003). Our experience has been that many undergraduate sociology students have been educated and trained in experimental and survey research, but not in field research. You may have had less education and training in case study and ethnographic strategies in your research methods classes. We review a few issues related to these latter studies, which are very common field studies in communities and organizations.

CASE STUDY RESEARCH

A **case study** is "systematically gathering enough information about a particular person, social setting, event, or group to permit the researcher to effectively understand how it operates or functions" (Berg 2001, 233), and it is usually done over a long period of time. A case study can provide the depth of understanding of the community, organization, process, or event. A careful description about a community can be very useful since it answers the questions of what happened, who was involved, what did they say, when did it occur, and identifying patterns of behavior.

A case study is one research strategy when people are interested in asking "how" and "why" questions, when they have little control over what is happening in the community, and when they are studying a contemporary, ongoing issue in the community (Yin 2003). Sometimes the case may be an individual, a group, organization, or community, or multiple cases. The idea is to provide an analysis of the context and processes involved in the phenomenon under study, not to isolate the phenomenon from its context as in other types of studies, for example a laboratory study (Hartley 1994).

Critical case studies analyze the structural arrangements and patterns found in organizations, groups, events, processes (Rossman and Rallis 1998, 70–71), or communities. For example, if you were doing a critical case study of a community you would generate adequate data to provide you with insights into the culture: how it is organized; patterns of human interactions; and how these are linked to broader social structures such as political systems, family systems, legal systems, power, inequality, and so on.

The value of theory is paramount in a case study, otherwise you end up with a great amount of description that has limited value beyond the case itself. It is important to connect observations with existing knowledge to broaden your perspective. Case studies begin with an idea and with a conceptual orientation that is broad and open-ended. The structure of the case study will draw from your previous knowledge, use of paradigms, and literature review, which we discuss in the section on using a conceptual framework. The theoretical orientation that you start out with may not be the same framework that you use in the entire study because you are engaged in building and generating theory throughout the research process.

While you may use several methods of data generation when doing a case study, including surveys, your main methods will often be participant observation and interviewing. Your basic data will be words, not numbers. These words come from your observations, interviews, field notes, documents, and books. Since words have multiple meanings, your critical approach and critical thinking skills will help to make sense of them in your analysis and interpretation.

Some examples of classic case studies include the following: *Middletown: A Study in American Culture* by H. Lynd and R. Lynd (1929); *Asylums* by E. Goffman (1961); and *Street Corner Society* by W. F. Whyte (1943). Whyte describes a subculture of lower-income youths that had not been frequently studied. He describes their ability and lack of ability to leave their neighborhood ties. This study is still useful to practicing sociologists as they work to understand the social and group structure of neighborhoods. A contemporary example of a case study is *Nickel and Dimed: On (Not) Getting By in America* (2001) by Barbara Ehrenreich.

ETHNOGRAPHY

Ethnographies are studies in which the researcher studies a cultural group in a natural setting. The core of ethnography is the meaning of actions and events to the people we seek to understand. These meanings may be expressed in language or be taken for granted and communicated only indirectly through words and action. We know that in every society, people make constant use of these complex meaning systems to organize their behavior. These systems constitute their culture. Moreover, an important idea of ethnography is that this type of research places people in the "midst of whatever it is they study" (Berg 2001, 134). Thus, it is important to know yourself. Review our discussion of discovering yourself in Chapter 3.

Critical ethnographies explore the structure and patterns of culture as used by one group to shape the actions of another group (Rossman and Rallis 1998, 67–69). If you were to do this type of ethnography, you would challenge the activities, policies, and other types of human interactions. You would question existing relationships and look at the issues from various perspectives.

> Critical ethnographers attempt to aid emancipatory goals, negate repressive influences, raise consciousness, and invoke a call to action that potentially will lead to social change. (Creswell 1994, 12)

The essential core of ethnography is the concern with the meanings of actions and events to the people in the community. Your basic data will consist of information about what people say (cultural knowledge), what they do (cultural behavior), and what they leave behind in the form of manufactured artifacts and documents (cultural artifacts).

After you have generated, organized, and analyzed all the data you need and want, your main task is interpretation of these data. Your analysis will tell the story about the community that is the focus of your research. For example, if you find that all homeless people in the community act in a certain manner and refuse a bed in the local shelter, you want to ask why. You may decide to do participant observation in the community to find out why many homeless persons in the community refuse to go into a shelter on a freezing cold night. Perhaps there is something missing from your observations and analysis that would help you understand this behavior. Are homeless people afraid of being hurt by other people in a shelter, or do they fear someone will steal the few personal belongings they have? When one of our students did such a study of homeless women, these were two of the major stories told by the homeless women to explain why they stayed away from the shelters unless they were truly desperate. Depending upon what you want to accomplish in your community study, you may extend your research to find answers to other questions such as what can be done about the problem.

We refer you to an ethnographic study, *Tell Them Who I Am: The Lives of Homeless Women* (1993) by Elliot Liebow. He describes a subculture of homeless women who have not been studied before. He describes their daily routines, how they cope with the problems of killing time for twelve hours a day when the shelter is closed to them, and how they deal with constant fatigue. But he also describes their strengths, how they use humor, and how they build friendships and care for one another. This study may be useful to you as you work to bring about change in how resources are used to address an increasing community problem.

Other ethnographies include: *Ain't No Makin' It* by Jay MacLeod (1995); *The Unknown City* by Michelle Fine and Lois Weis (1998); *Teen Mothers* by Ruth Horowitz (1996); and *Code of the Street: Decency, Violence, and the Moral Life of the Inner City* by Elijah Anderson (2000). The most classic of ethnographies is one you may have read in your introductory sociology course, *Tally's Corner: A Study of Negro Streetcorner Men* (1967), by Elliott Liebow. Both critical ethnographies and critical case studies provide the bases for understanding social phenomena in a way that allows for the application of the findings to pursuing social justice.

PLANNING YOUR COMMUNITY PROJECT

Planning a research project may be one of the many challenging tasks of your university education. We hope that early in your program you recorded in your journal your goals and objectives so that you will be generating data to answer some of these questions. As you make these decisions, write them down in your journal. Doing this helps you to recognize your biases and how these may have influenced your work. It is important that you be able to review these steps in your decision making when you do your analysis and interpretation. In this section, we provide you with some guidelines to complete this task.

SELECTING YOUR RESEARCH TOPIC

You need to plan early on where you will do your fieldwork in your community-based learning program, a decision that is generally made with the help of your professor. Depending upon the type of course you are taking (e.g., internship, service-learning, or others), you may be limited in the degree to which you can become a full participant in the community. The availability of opportunities in a community and access to community members will also shape the type of project you can do. In such situations, you may need to develop your own project without community assistance and guidance. However, you can adapt field research methods to meet your own needs and goals. Whatever you choose to do, it is important that you have clear guidance from your professor. Ask questions for clarity and assistance in getting started.

You may find it difficult to select an issue to study if this is your first experience with community and field work. There is much to study at your fieldwork site. Looking over your journal should make this readily apparent. For those of you who are unsure of how to get started in your research or how to select a topic, interview a few people who are knowledgeable about your interests and who are likely to give you a sense of direction. This includes interviewing your professor, who may already have a community project going. It takes time to develop a project and carry it out. If you can piggyback on an existing project the first time, you may experience less frustration than when you create your own. Another source is to look at your university or college directory for the different programs and organizations on campus that are engaged in promoting community support.

What should you consider when selecting a research topic? First, you want to select a topic that you find interesting; one where you will learn and expand your critical thinking; and one that is important to others in the community. You are going to spend many hours working on this project; it is best if you are interested. Your learning opportunities will be enhanced if you believe the project is worth doing or the issue is important to you. Second, you have to ask yourself if the topic is doable in the amount of time you have to complete this project, and if it is feasible. It is not easy to structure a community study within an academic semester (Strand et al. 2003).

Third, some topics may best be avoided. If you are too emotionally close to a topic it may be difficult to look at all perspectives. For example, someone with HIV may find it difficult to explore the political aspects of drug testing. If you feel so strongly that poor people are poor because they are lazy and do not want to work, it may be difficult to explore and hear their stories. In addition, you might do more harm than good without realizing that your biases are showing in the questions you ask or how you interpret the data.

Fourth, keep in mind that your research topic may change as you spend more time at your field site. An important point to think about when you choose your research topic is to "start where you are." What arouses your curiosity so that you want to know more about an idea or social relationship? What do you care about enough to spend a semester exploring it? If you see yourself as different from others because of ethnic, racial, or sexual identity, you may be interested in enlarging your perspective to examine how your view is shaped by social forces and social structure.

Who you are, your values and beliefs, all play a key part in the selection process. Because of this, it is so important to use critical thinking discussed in Chapter 2 so you do not confound your research findings with your own personal assumptions and biases. You have your beliefs, which are reflected in an ideological lens. You use this lens to look at the issues you want to study, the data you generate, and how you interpret your data. Thus, your research is never value neutral. What is important is that you acknowledge your own personal interests and biases. We hope you have recorded these in your journal.

Here is an example of a project you might consider. You are interested in homeless families because you have seen them while traveling in several cities. You have found from your reading that there is little known about these families, but you have read in the newspaper that the number of homeless families is increasing rapidly. You are curious to know if this is the case and why it would be so. You select an urban setting where you think homeless families may be living on the street or in shelters. In your preliminary investigation, you learn that there are very few shelters that take women and their children. You may have to modify your research question at this point. You decide to continue your ministudy but you have difficulty finding families in shelters since there are few shelters that take families. What strategies will you use to continue your study? Perhaps you can find a not-for-profit organization that might have some information that would further your effort. One source of value to you would be the National Coalition for the Homeless. See http://nch.ari.net. You might also want to read the ethnography we mentioned earlier: *Tell Them Who I Am: The Lives of Homeless Women* (Liebow 1993). As you read this, write down what you consider to be Liebow's conceptual framework. Do not concentrate on the findings but how he explains the strategies he chose to use in his research. Write down his research questions and approaches to answering these. You will learn why he had to modify his strategies during his study.

USING A CONCEPTUAL FRAMEWORK

After you have decided on your general topic of interest, the conceptual framework is the next major step in your research process. Remember, selecting a topic of interest is different from selecting how you are going to study it with some conceptual framework. Next, identify what your research is about and your research questions. This includes the use of relevant literature and paradigms that guide what you are going to explore, including relevant concepts and logic of inquiry. It is in your best interest to begin thinking about your conceptual framework early on in your community-based learning program, even though you will find it necessary to make changes as you move forward. For some of you this will be a new experience; others may already be part of an ongoing community project before you read the literature. Review Chapter 2 on the topics of sociological perspectives and concepts to help you get started.

We prefer to use the idea of a *conceptual* framework instead of a *theoretical* framework as a guide for you, although you will learn about theorizing later in this chapter. Some of you have not had enough experience using theories or reading about them in your studies. You have, however, been grounded in sociological concepts throughout your training. For example, you may have learned that law is one of the most significant institutions of social control today. You may want to study how laws have affected housing for the homeless. Laws may be federal, state, and local, and these do shape housing availability for all ages and economic groups. If you are working with the community to study some aspect of homelessness, you may want to educate the community on the many levels of laws that determine what housing is available now and is planned for the future. One source you would want to look into if you decided to continue your study is the Community Data and On-Line Resources at http://www.accra.org/research_data/commdata.htm, discussed later in this chapter.

You could learn about local zoning laws that restrict affordable housing units in certain communities. You could work with community members to initiate action to have these zoning regulations changed. For example, a group of community members could go to the local government to determine when zoning hearings are held. They could take their views to the county officials who are responsible for making local ordinance decisions. This would be a beginning step for everyone to take action to create change in a community.

We hope that you and the community will collaborate on projects that will be of benefit to everyone's learning and to promoting social justice. Remember, your sociological concepts will be important during your entire fieldwork experience. Hopefully, you have written these primary concepts in your journal in the memo section, and you revisit these memos frequently.

Use of Literature

When you start your project, you will want to investigate what is known on your topic. However, you probably will not know all the possible bodies of literature that might provide you with ideas to start your research. One way to approach the sociological literature is to find one or two books written on the research topic you have chosen and write a book review of each book. In your review, you would summarize the main topic of the book, the specific issues in the book that may be related to your research topic, the key findings, and proposed solutions and recommendations if these are provided. Next, you would apply a critical thinking approach to your reading and explain in your own words the major research ideas in the book. Can you pick out the perspective that the author is using and the strategies the author uses to answer the major research issues? Consider whether you think the author was biased in any way when doing the study, in the analysis or in the interpretations. We realize these are difficult questions but we want you to be critical of what you read rather than just summarizing a book. Be sure you understand how being critical is different from criticizing. You may want to discuss this idea in class since these processes are often confused. Write these thoughts in your journal so that you can refresh yourself at the end of the semester on the journey you have taken.

Another practice that may be helpful is to read book reviews in *Contemporary Sociology* to get an idea how to write one. Limiting your literature search to one journal will prevent you from becoming overwhelmed. Another source for literature review is the Internet. If you find no one has written about your topic in the journals, then you would need to broaden your search to other sources. A good source for you to review is James Shiveley and Phillip VanFossen, *Using INTERNET Primary Sources to Teach Critical Thinking Skills in Government, Economics, and Contemporary World Issues* (2001).

Use of Paradigms

In your sociology classes, you learned about paradigms. You read a brief review in Chapter 2 of paradigms that sociologists find useful in explaining the social world. Many of you probably wondered how paradigms would be of any use to you. They are important to understand when you do field research. Reflect on how your beliefs about truth, reality, and human agency shape the way you select your research project and the questions you want to answer. These views and the assumptions you make regarding these questions will shape the research strategies and methods you choose. These beliefs will also shape the development of your conceptual framework.

It is important that you reflect on what you believe constitutes truth and how you know it. Do you assume there is a single truth or do you believe there are multiple perspectives regarding the social world? Is evidence only that which is determined scientifically or can evidence come from many places, including emotions, intuition, and so forth? Furthermore, you need to reflect on what you think is the nature of reality. Is it something that is out there, independent of humans? As we practice sociology can we uncover the "facts and processes that constitute that reality" (Rossman and Rallis 1998, 31)? Or are social processes and facts a matter of interpretation and thus not independent of human's conceptions? It is important for you to know whether you believe that the nature of reality is independent of human beings or subjective.

Your views on human agency will also shape how you interpret your data and thus your theoretical explanations. We like the question that Russell Crescimanno (1991) uses to engage his students in critical thinking about human agency. He asks his students "What does it mean to be human" (Crescimanno 1991, 12)? He asks ". . . the student-as-human not to take human being-ness for granted but to consider it, instead, in light of the material at hand. This interruption of the taken-for granted-world of the student is at the heart of the critical thinking process" (12).

We ask you to do the same when you consider your belief as to whether people have free will or are programmed to respond in some predetermined manner. Or do you believe that humans are active and creative beings who make choices unfettered by the social world in which they live? So before you begin your observations and study you need to write down your beliefs on several important assumptions that will shape your ability to do field research. Record these in your journal so that you can reflect on them later. You may find your beliefs changing during the semester if you become involved in social advocacy.

When you are doing observations in the community or listening to women tell you about their experiences during lunch at a soup kitchen, you will react differently depending on the assumptions you make about human nature. If you hold the view that people who do not work are lazy and thus should not receive assistance from the community, you may not be able to hear or listen carefully to what homeless people are telling you. You may not be able to hear their stories if they tell you they are not paid enough money to be able to live like other people do. You may be judging them on the basis of individual factors because you cannot move beyond your own beliefs and assumptions, especially if you see these same people at the same soup kitchens daily. If you find yourself judging these people instead of trying to understand the connections among these patterns, you would find it helpful to apply a critical thinking approach that would expand your way of knowing so you can accept that there are many ways to know—so you would keep your mind open when you see the same patterns at the food service. Look at what you believe and how you came to believe it. Do the facts support what you believe? Critical thinkers avoid weak arguments based only on what they believe to be fact. Perhaps it would be helpful to look beyond the discovered facts and see the connections among the facts.

One way to increase your reflective space would be to review some sociological theories that have been useful in explaining homeless behavior. If you are interested in structural explanations, as we hope you will be, then reading *Children on the Streets of the Americas* (2000) by Roslyn Mickelson will help you learn how poverty is structured into the economies of many cities. There may be no opportunities for people to work for adequate wages to support themselves. There may not be an adequate supply of low-cost housing or enough homes for everyone in the community. For example, you could check the numbers of homes and apartments in most communities by going to the community data bases we mentioned earlier. Such information should help to shape how you view the problem of homelessness.

You might also want to read *Keeping Women and Children Last: America's War on the Poor* (1996) by Ruth Sidel. She describes how people who are labeled the "underclass," who are seen as irredeemable, lazy, single women and welfare recipients, are known as the "enemy within" (1996, 1). If this sounds familiar to you and comfortable as an explanation for homeless women's behavior, then you will need to open your mind to alternative structural explanations. You need to question the assumptions behind many of these beliefs, including your own.

The use of paradigms to expand your critical thinking is invaluable. It will encourage you to look for another view and the reasoning behind another view. By taking another view, you are forced to read and think and challenge your personal beliefs. Critical thinking will help you decide what you see, as does the guidance of a paradigm. These will also help you to learn how to identify propaganda and logical fallacies. In doing so, you will have greater understanding of what Karl Marx was credited with writing: "Practice must seek its theory."

FIELD RESEARCH

Research is a process of discovery, whether in the field or in a laboratory. However, even though you may be generating data in the field, it does not follow that you are doing fieldwork. Doing fieldwork requires a level of involvement by the researcher that is different from generating data only. It means participation in some activities often over time, and it means that you keep field notes. We separate our discussion into fieldwork and field notes to permit more focused discussion on each topic, while acknowledging there is overlap in these topics.

FIELDWORK

Fieldwork has been described as ". . . gathering information through observations, interviews, and materials helpful in developing a portrait and establishing 'cultural rules' of the culture-sharing group" (Creswell 1998, 60). It is generally accepted that the goal of fieldwork is to recognize patterns. Two basic problems of fieldwork are figuring out what data to get and what to do with the data you get (Wolcott 1995). Fieldwork can be an exhilarating, exciting experience and a meaningful learning experience. It is not a new experience for you.

We all act as ordinary participants in a variety of social situations. Once we learn the cultural rules, the rules become tacit and we think little about what we are doing. A simple and fun way to begin thinking about fieldwork is to recall how you learned about the culture of college life after you arrived with your parents, unpacked, and moved into your new housing arrangements with new roommates. You were in a new culture, a new field, although you came to the situation with many preconceived notions, experiences, theories, and dreams about college life. You had to learn about new rules, rituals, norms, and many other necessary elements of college life. This is the process of **cultural acquisition** in which you ask yourself, what do I have to know in order to learn about the culture of this college campus? How do I learn it?

So basically you began to "hang out" with new people, going to new places, asking questions, listening to others' conversations, making observations about your environment, particularly where you find food and laundry facilities. You were doing fieldwork in this situation. You were watching people, talking to people, reflecting on what they said, and looking for some patterns and consistencies that generated data for analysis and interpretation. You were learning the culture and determining where you fit into it by **funneling,** making decisions about which data to get more of, and how to use data already at hand (Wolcott 1995, 385).

Throughout your experiences you were concerned with how you presented yourself to the other students (Goffman 1959). You may have imagined and planned how to behave around these new people, or you may not have been self-conscious about your field experience. While you do not write a formal research report on this learning experience, you may have called your friends at other colleges, or sent an e-mail message to your parents or friends explaining what you had learned, and how this fit in with your preconceived ideas. You probably made some decisions as well, for example, do you buy a meal card in a dormitory or eat wherever other students hang out. However, your decision may be shaped by outside forces such as being subject to negotiation with your parents who have their own ideas. Your decision may also be subject to your available financial resources, as well as those of your parents.

When you are participating in a community-based learning program, you will be learning through the same process as described above. You are entering a new field, trying to understand the rituals, rules, norms, and connections among the people in the field. You are studying the culture that involves cultural knowledge, behavior, and artifacts (Spradley 1980).

FIELD NOTES

A field note has been described as "an ongoing stream-of-consciousness commentary about what is happening in the research, involving both observation and analysis—preferably separated from one another" (Huber and VandeVen, citing Van

Maanen 1995, 74). Another view on field notes states that the way you turn what you see and hear into data is by writing field notes (Rossman and Rallis 1998, 137). They argue that field notes have two major components: the descriptive data of what you observe, and your comments on these data. They call this the *running record,* in which you include as much detail as possible about the physical environment, and the activities and interactions among the people. The second component is your commentary on that record, *observer comments,* including your emotional reactions to events, analytic insights, questions about meaning, and thoughts for modifying your design.

Keeping field notes is a rigorous task and "what the write-up is to intensive interviewing, field notes are to participant observation: the crucial data log out of which the analysis will emerge" (Lofland and Lofland 1995, 89). We mentioned in Chapter 4 that you might be making mental field notes, jotted notes, and full field notes. The mental and jotted notes are not field notes until you have changed these to a running log of observations.

When doing field research, there are several methods for generating data in a community or organization. We examine three: participant observation, interviewing, and collecting documents and artifacts. Often these methods are used concomitantly, for example, in order to improve on the accuracy of your observations, you may want to supplement observation with an interview.

PARTICIPANT OBSERVATION

Katherine DeWalt and Billie DeWalt in *Participant Observation, A Guide for Field-workers* (2002) write that participant observation has become a common feature of qualitative research in a number of disciplines. The underlying assumption is that you gain a greater understanding of the phenomena under study if you study this from the point of view of the participants. "A good part of what makes up the method of participant observation, both the collection of information and analysis, is difficult to put into words. In part, it is because this is a method in which *control* of the research situation is less in the hands of the investigator than with other methods . . ." (2002, vii). When you are generating ethnographic data using participant observation, you are reacting to and interacting with others. The researcher has less opportunity to influence data generation than with a structured interview.

An essential means of gathering ethnographic data is observing (i.e., looking and listening). It is a process whereby you describe what is going on, who is involved in the interaction, the context in which the interactions occur, how they occur, and why, from the standpoint of the participants. It is a method that requires you to share the experiences of those from whom you learn. Rather than studying people in the community, people are your teachers. They are learning from you as well. It is an iterative process.

Another way to describe participant observation is "the process in which an investigator establishes and sustains a many-sided and relatively long term relationship with a human association in its natural setting for the purpose of developing a scientific understanding of that association" (Lofland and Lofland 1995, 18). It is not always easy to do this type of observation because you will gain only a rather crude idea of the insider's world until you comprehend the *culture* and *language* that is used to communicate meanings. Remember we discussed these concepts in Chapter 3.

Participant Observer Research Roles

One of the most important decisions you will need to make when doing participant observation is what role would be appropriate to the organization or community you are studying, and whether it is one that you can physically and emotionally accomplish. We discussed the concept of role in Chapter 3. There are at least four possible roles that researchers may enact when doing participant observation:

1. Complete participant
2. Participant-as-observer
3. Observer-as-participant
4. Complete observer (Cassell and Symon 1994, 108, citing Burgess's description)

Each of these roles will depend on what data you need to generate and your available resources to do this. For some of you this is a new way to generate data and the roles provide a guide to help you choose appropriate roles for your study. In each role, the degree of participation varies. You may need to practice doing the exercise on participant observation at the end of the chapter by yourself or with a friend so that you feel comfortable in the field.

In the **complete participant** role you conceal any intention to observe the setting. For example, you may want to study drinking behavior of college students in the student lounge. You could do this as a complete participant, never mentioning to your friends what you are doing, as long as you are at least twenty-one years of age. You would be working as a covert researcher. Thus, there would be no reason to ask for informed consent from your friends. However, you would be careful to protect your friends, withholding any personal identity when you do your analysis and report writing. You would also use pseudo names when you recorded your field notes.

If you were to do this study as **participant-as-observer,** different rules would be followed. The emphasis is on participation, rather than observation. You would probably drink with your friends in the role of **participant,** form relationships with them, but you would step back periodically to act as an **observer.** You would not hide your intentions from your friends or respondents and you may need to ask their consent. You would need to record in your field notes the specific times you were observing and times you were participating. When you do your analysis and interpretation, you need to identify which role you were playing and when.

In the third role, **observer-as-participant,** you would have very superficial relationships with your friends. The emphasis is on observation, rather than participation. You would participate very little, perhaps stepping back now and then to ask a few questions. In this situation, it could be argued that you need to inform people they are being observed and notes taken on their behavior. However, when you are in a public place there is less obligation to request consent from the people you are observing.

In the last role, **observer,** you are observing only. In the example we are using it might be difficult to stand back and "eavesdrop" on the drinking patterns of your friends without them becoming suspicious or annoyed. However, if you are doing this research in a public place, you have less obligation to inform them of your research.

As a fieldworker you will find it helpful to achieve some workable balance between participating and observing. This balance will likely be related to the project you have set up and the knowledge you need to obtain. Regardless of the role that you play, however, it is likely that your presence will have some impact on those you are observing. Be aware of this potential bias and make notes in your journal for when you are doing your analysis.

One description of a field worker is "someone who is blessed with a thick enough skin and an ability to depend consistently on their own initiative" (Waddington 1994, 120). If you are uncomfortable or inexperienced in taking initiative in social settings or "hanging out" in strange environments, you may find it difficult to use participant observation as a method. Learning how to do participant observation takes considerable practice.

Also, field research can be physically tiring and mentally wearying to the observer. Everything you are observing is likely to be strange, yet you must accommodate yourself to this. You will be introduced to a new culture, possibly a new language, or at least a variant of the language you are familiar with. You may feel a sense of being overwhelmed as you meet many new people, and are subject to great challenges in your tasks and social interactions as a participant. We caution you to remember our suggestions in Chapter 4 on recording and reflecting: Keep a small notebook in your pocket so that you can jot down notes as you have the opportunity. Do not wait until you leave the field site or get back to your apartment or dormitory. It will be too late, as first impressions only happen once.

INTERVIEWING

Many people think that interviewing is a simple task, and they do not need to read anything about it nor practice doing this. After all, they do it every day. However, when you are doing research in a community, your approach to interviewing will probably become focused on obtaining specific information that can be transformed into data. **Qualitative interviewing** is described as in-depth, semistructured, or loosely structured forms of interviewing (Mason 2002). Some characterize it as "conversations with a purpose." The goal of semistructured interviewing is to find out what kinds of things exist in the first place. But it is important when you begin an interview that you inform the person about your credentials, what the interview is about, what you are going to do with the information, and if you will treat the information as confidential (Keats 2000).

Before you begin your interview, reflect on the following set of questions:

1. How am I going to introduce myself and explain what I would like to do? In a community-based learning program, you will probably introduce yourself as a student taking a course at a university or college. You would need to be prepared to show some student identification if you are asked. You may under some circumstances be asked to bring a letter from the university stating who you are and what your purpose is. In our experience of teaching in this area, many of our students have been asked to provide the professor's name, telephone number, and some letter of identification.

2. How much do I tell the person being interviewed without biasing their responses? There is no correct answer to this question because we can not measure how much is likely to lead to bias. But your common sense should tell you that a general statement about your interests and concerns would be adequate. For example, you have read that many people who are retired are unable to live on their pensions and have to work part-time to meet their expenses. This is a surprise to you because from your observations, older retired people are doing fine, just like your grandparents and their friends. After you have located the people you are going to interview, you need to tell them why you, as a young student, want to talk with them. You could tell them you are interested in how retired people are getting along in the community and how they are adjusting to retirement. That is a general statement that should prompt their interest. It does not suggest that they are not getting along but during the course of the interview you can ask more specific questions that relate to economic hardship if this does not come out in the interview.

3. How do I arouse their interest? Tell them why this topic is of interest to you and why you think it is important to understand. This may be difficult to explain to people who are at least two generations older than you. You had better write down how you became interested in this topic and practice your explanation with your friends. Often we become curious because we recognize a discrepancy between what we expected on some issue and what we observed. So if this is the case, there will be a way you can work this into your introduction.

4. How will I close the interview? It is usually a good idea to alert the person you are interviewing that you are almost at the end of the interview and the time allotted to complete it. Daphne Keats (2000) suggests that you gradually wind down the interview rather than an abrupt end so that you leave the person with a sense of satisfaction. When you finish the interview, both you and the person you are talking with should feel that you have done something worth doing. (Keats 2000, 50)

These questions on the interview process are quite important and you will probably benefit from writing out your answers to these questions. Have someone in your class, and/or your professor read these answers. Ask them for feedback that you can use to improve your interviewing skills.

One way to start your interview is with a short list of issue-oriented questions developed from your review of the literature or early interviews with community members. These interview questions are likely to be open-ended rather than closed-ended. When you ask an open-ended question you are asking the person to share with you their understanding of the question and issue. So when people who are poor are asked to describe what it means to be poor, they are answering from what they feel and know. You have not imposed any limitations on their view of the issue by giving them a set of predetermined categories to choose from. If you were asking a closed-ended question, the people would have to make a choice from the categories you have preselected for them. When doing a survey and using a questionnaire, you are more interested in controlling the questions and topics covered. You would probably use closed-ended questions where people who answer the questions have limited choices to select.

Perhaps you may want to give a copy of the questions to the person you are interviewing. You want to get in-depth responses and descriptions of whatever you are probing. It is often a good idea to try out the questions, even if in a mental rehearsal. But it would probably help you more if you practiced your interview on a friend or classmate to get important feedback on how you are doing. It is important to develop your interview and speaking skills before you go into the field with your research.

During the actual interview, you need most to listen, maybe take few or many notes, but to stay in control of the data gathering, thinking about what form the account will take in writing.

The words spoken during an interview are not the only data that result from an interview but they *are* data . . . they can be sorted and labeled, and they lend themselves superbly to a search for repetitions, regularities, schemata, themes, aberrations, paradoxes, problems, turnings. (Wolcott 1995, 385)

You may find that developing an interview guide, carrying out interviews, and analyzing transcripts are all highly time-consuming activities. You need to be careful that you allow adequate time for all of the processes.

Finally, if you have little experience with this form of data generation and it is the main method you will use, practice before you begin your work. Practice in front of a mirror, with your friends, or use a video camera. Listen to what you hear and see from those who are trying to help you. When you start your study, you want to be certain that your skill as an interviewer is adequate to complete the task.

DOCUMENTS AND ARTIFACTS

Documents are evidence of the material culture of the community and organization. When you are doing fieldwork for the first time, you may feel comfortable collecting a wide range of documents. Often people in the field will give you documents to use, such as brochures, reports, and rosters to familiarize yourself with the organization or community. Also, there will be times when supporting documents and visual data may be important to your study purposes. This will depend on the context of your study. For example, it would be useful in your community-based learning program to have a copy of the table of organization, and the mission of the organization in which you are observing. It would also be useful to know the types of occupations employed by the organization, as well as the proposed budget. These are all text-based documents.

There may be one drawback to collecting many documents since these are often long and may need clarification and summarizing. You need to know the document's significance (i.e., what the document tells you and others about the site that is important). One way to organize your documents is to create a document summary form for each document, which can be coded for later analysis (Miles and Huberman 1994). Include in this form some of the following: date document received, document number, name and description of document, event or contact with which the document is associated, significance or importance of document, and brief summary of the contents. You may want to code these summary forms for easy retrieval later, or for further analysis.

Community Data and On-Line Resources for Researchers

When you are doing a community project, there may be times when you need other data to help you put your study in context, for comparison purposes, or to help community members use and interpret statistics. We provide you with some examples of Web-based community resources and encourage you to search for others. You can find these by searching http://www.accra.org/research_data/commdata.htm. ACCRA is a nonprofit organization promoting excellence in research for community and economic development.

There are many standardized data sources provided by federal government agencies that you may want to investigate. We caution you to use critical thinking when you are using these data sources and to look for the possible sources of bias and error contained within them. Here are a few examples: the Bureau of Labor Statistics, the Bureau of Justice Statistics, the Census Bureau, the National Center for Education Statistics, and the National Center for Health Statistics. For example, the Census Bureau provides data on demographic and economic state and county profiles. These data may be useful when you are theorizing and developing structural explanations in your community study or when you want to strengthen your arguments on an advocacy issue. If you are studying welfare reform, you will be interested in the Urban Institute's New Federalism Project. The database, "Assessing the New Federalism," is the most complete research that is publicly available via the Internet. It provides a comprehensive database including all states and the District of Columbia to determine and compare state performance in welfare, social programs, poverty, and development.

MAKING SENSE OF YOUR DATA

Once you and the community have thought through the conceptual framework, you have entered the field, and you are recording field notes, decisions about analyzing the data become paramount. A basic characteristic of field research is that data generation and data analysis do not proceed in linear progression. Instead, you proceed simultaneously through a process of coding, one of the most essential features of field research, and more data generation. Coding entails reviewing your data and taking it apart meaningfully while keeping the relations between the parts intact. It requires you to organize your many sources of data into some manageable form. It requires you to systematically review your data in a disciplined way. In this section, we address some of the issues of analysis including coding, developing themes, reflecting, and theorizing.

CODING

If you are going to practice sociology in the community you need to have at least a basic understanding of the major issues in the analytic process of coding. For example, you may collect a huge amount of data that you will need to organize and analyze. To do that, you need to have a minimal understanding of how to code your data. In the text that follows we discuss what coding is, what a code is, how to code, and why we should code.

What Is Coding?

Coding is analysis. The process of **coding** is one of the most essential features of the field research. It is an **iterative** (i.e., repetitious) process and involves organizing data into categories related to the framework and questions guiding the study. Coding is used to support analysis and interpretation. You are tagging data and putting these into categories to be used in helping you find patterns and themes. Categories are concepts and abstractions that are vague and ephemeral. Your task is to make them concrete through snippets and segments of data.

When you are coding you have to think through what you take as evidence of a category or theme (Rossman and Rallis 1998), so you need to be clear about the words or phrases that illustrate each of the concepts. You need to handle the words carefully. If you are studying homelessness, what would you take as evidence of homelessness? What constitutes evidence of a category should be grounded in the data (Rossman and Rallis 1998, 180). By this we mean that when you are organizing your data into categories, you are not imposing these on the data. The data are telling you what the categories are and should be.

We suggest to our students that they begin coding after they have written their first memo, observation, or interview. Hopefully, you will be coding and recoding during your entire research project. Since this is likely to be a new experience for you, we encourage you to code your data more than once. Recoding will stimulate new ideas and new codes or the collapsing of some former codes.

It is a challenging and time consuming effort to come up with categories and labels that can have multiple definitions, but with a common theme. Here is where bias comes into the process. Also, each individual will code the data differently, so their coding of the data will vary. But remember, as long you make clear how and why you have developed your codes, someone can replicate your work or check your work to see that you are consistent. That is the yardstick used to determine validity in your coding.

What Is a Code?

A **code** is a name or symbol that stands for a group of similar items or phenomena that you have observed in your data set. Codes are efficient data-labeling and data-retrieval devices. Codes are tags or labels of assigning units of meaning to the descriptive information you generated during your study. For example, in a study on learning to work, LeCompte used the code word "Time" to refer to deadlines, schedules, time limits, being on time, or the specific time of day (LeCompte and Schensul 1999, 55).

One result of coding your data is the creation of less data as the data are coded, counted, and summarized. In this example, a considerable amount of data is reduced to one code, time. Some codes are easy to recognize, especially if you are pursuing an issue of passionate interest to you so that you are knowledgeable about the issue. From reading and coursework you should be able to analyze your field notes by creating codes. The knowledge from your course work and reading is important when you are doing your coding analysis. Also, if you are doing a community project where members are involved in many stages of the research, then they will likely wish to engage in the organization and analysis of the data (Strand et al. 2003). " . . . it is the community members' perspective, and their potential for acting on the analysis, that brings perhaps the most distinctive contribution to the collaborative research process" (2003, 113).

How to Code

One way to begin the coding process is to first create a provisional "start list" that derives from your initial conceptual framework, research questions, and other key features that you bring to the study (Miles and Huberman 1994, 58). While there are many schemes for beginning the coding process, one point is important to remember: Codes will change and develop as fieldwork continues. For example, one student studying the perceptions of refugees and asylum seekers making job transitions in the United States wrote the following in his paper:

> *I think the codes should be "loose." That is, they should be viewed iteratively several times. By coding my data, I intend to create categories as references that are "unfinished." By that I mean that codes are something like clue markers. While a coded piece of data might have similarities to another similarly coded piece, it is important to recognize that such similar pieces are not identical pieces. There are codes that seem to intersect, and there are codes that seem too "slippery" to assign to one category.*

If you spend much time doing field research you will become familiar with revising your codes. Some codes do not work and others get revised, since no field materials fit into the code.

Sociologist Anselm Strauss (1993, 27–28) suggests a **coding paradigm** that includes the following: conditions, interaction among the actors, strategies and tactics, and consequences. This paradigm may be of use to you as a new researcher. When you are looking for conditions, look for words and phrases such as the following: "because," "since," or "on account of." When you are looking for consequences, look for words and phrases such as the following: "as a result," "because of," "the result was," "the consequence was," and "in consequence." Strauss notes that strategies are more direct and easy to identify. He characterizes interactions as occurring among actors, rather than use of strategies and tactics. Strauss argues that without the coding paradigm items, coding is not coding.

You will find that some codes will be more obvious to you than others. This can be explained by looking at your background, your course of studies, the topics of interest to you and other factors. We like what we know, and we remember what we know, what interests us, and is familiar to us. This is a good time to review the courses you have taken and to think about the major concepts and theories that remained with you after you left the classroom or finished the course. Here is a place where the community and university are bridged and you can make a contribution to the community with the knowledge you have.

Types of Coding   There are several ways you can code your data. We discuss open and axial coding only. When you are doing **open coding** of your data, you are engaged in unrestricted coding. You begin by looking very closely at your field notes, interviews, and other data you have generated. Drawing upon your sociological perspective, you are trying to produce concepts that appear to fit your data. This assumes that you have clarified your perspective early in your project. These may not be the perspective or concepts that you end up using but they will start you thinking of alternative views and explanations. Strauss lists a few guidelines to use when studying the data and doing open coding:

1. Ask a general question of the data such as, what study are these data pertinent to? This alerts you to the possibility that the original idea may be modified. Ask frequently what category or property of a category the incident indicates, and what part of the emerging theory it indicates.
2. It is important to analyze the data minutely. As we noted earlier, analysis means breaking data into parts and reassembling them. This is important so you do not miss any new ideas and so that you prepare for developing well-integrated theory, rather than impressionistic theory.
3. Periodically you need to stop the coding process and write a theoretical memo. Strauss argues this moves you more quickly from the data and into analysis and seeing patterns that can be used for selecting themes. (30–32)

Finally, Strauss notes the following:

> The point is really that the potential is not so much in the document as in the relationship between it and the inquiring mind and training of a researcher who vigorously and imaginatively engages in the open coding. (1993, 28)

The purpose of open coding is to open up the mind and inquiry. Thus, each interpretation is a tentative one. What is important is that coding is grounded in the data. However, remember that you are putting the data into categories so your interpretation is a key factor in your analysis. It is how you interpret what is in the field notes and prepare it into codes that become the data for analysis. Interpretation in field research can be a source of bias and error.

The student studying the perceptions of refugees and asylum seekers in the United States described his view on interpretation this way:

> *One of the texts mentioned that I should code more literally at first and then get into interpretation slowly. I'm not sure I agree with this sentiment.*

I immediately began coding interpretatively, and I think this can be important since first impressions are nuanced and can disappear from memory. There are certain interpretations a researcher can make based on intuition. I think this is good, as long as the researcher examines the empirical reasons for the interpretation. There will always be at least some question as to whether or not the interpretation is accurate.

Another form of coding is axial coding, which is essentially a part of the open coding. When you are using this form of coding, you are doing an intense analysis around one category at a time, in terms of the paradigm Strauss developed. It is called axis coding because your analysis revolves around the "axis" of one category at a time (Strauss 1993, 32). This type of coding is usually done later in the coding process when you have identified more clearly what categories are important.

No matter how you decide to do your coding, you will eventually need to develop a codebook in which you define the codes as clearly as possible so that others can understand your definitions and categories quickly and easily. A codebook is a list of all the codes used for the analysis of a particular collection of data. Codebooks are created once a coding system has been devised and more or less finalized. You will learn when doing field research that analytic tasks almost never are completely finished. What we have found useful in helping our students develop a codebook is to have them prepare a list of the following: (1) list the research questions you started with; (2) list any modifications to the research question and when these occurred; (3) list your coding categories and all the options available for each code; (4) list several examples illustrating the kinds of units or behaviors that fit into the category. It is useful to devise a set of criteria delineating the characteristics that should be present in a unit before it is coded with a particular code.

We continue using an example from the student mentioned earlier studying occupational transition among refugees in the United States.

I found coding my data to be much more complicated than I expected. It takes a lot of time and clear logic. Even with three interviews to analyze, I reworked my codebook for a solid month before arriving at the final version.

This student developed three iterations of his codebook. The early iteration represented preliminary ideas and concepts. These included six major categories, including a miscellaneous category. With one exception, these categories contained from one to four codes, for a total of fifteen codes. He expanded the next iteration of his codebook since more issues kept arising, for example, in the education category. In addition, he added a family category with emphasis on family values and a cultural adaptation category, for a total of twenty-six.

The last iteration of the codebook included thirty codes. The category "cultural adaptation" contained nine codes, the highest in any category. The category "family" began with two codes and was expanded to six in the final version. Two of the categories, "individualism" and "family values," were not expected when he began his study. One category, "physical challenges," contained fewer codes in the final iteration of the codebook.

Our students found it helpful to keep their codebook on their computer so that when it was modified, they had previous copies and could evaluate why they made changes. Your codebook is your own creation and thus will be different from others. But as long as you include the items listed above, others can follow how you did your work.

Jay MacLeod (1995) does an excellent job of describing the process he went through in his field research entitled *Ain't No Makin' It*. He notes how he tried many ways to make sense of his data.

I highlighted the interviews using a complex color-coded scheme. Sally created a one-page index on each youth with crucial information. I developed intricate outlines, made reams of notes, created subject indexes, and distilled whole interviews down to a single sheet of paper. Reading the texts of the chapters now, I find it all seems so simple and straightforward. It wasn't. (MacLeod 1995, 301–302)

Why Code?

As we mentioned earlier in the gathering data section of this chapter, the information you generate through field notes, documents, and interviews piles up geometrically. You have to be able to present your findings in summary form instead of pages of notes and descriptions. As a newcomer to field research, you may experience early on in your project an eagerness to collect everything that might be relevant or not relevant. Thus, you may need to find another place besides your room to store everything.

But remember, data generation is a **selective** process. You cannot and will not "get it all" even though you may think you can. To avoid the possibility of data overload we suggest that you keep firmly in mind the purpose of your study and why you are doing it. One of the best defenses against data overload is to revisit your conceptual framework and research questions frequently. Too often researchers write down their framework and purposes and forget them during their study. You need to visit them frequently throughout your entire study.

Your research questions are most important when it comes to your coding work. Coding will help you reduce the amount of information you have generated into a manageable amount. It will speed up the time to do further analysis by providing you with patterns that are emerging, and it may need to be reviewed in other data you have collected. Another value of coding is that it allows you to evaluate the field data in terms of common themes, issues, and trends and to discover how the data generated either support or refute your assumptions. Also, coding can demonstrate where data may be missing in your study so that you can go back into the field promptly.

DEVELOPING THEMES

Now that you have organized your data and selected categories that are as inclusive as possible, use those categories to help you find the meaning of your findings. You have carefully looked for the evidence in each category and now you examine how these categories are linked, perhaps as themes. Margot Ely, in *Doing Qualitative Research, Circles within Circles* (1991), defines themes as either of the following:

1. A statement of meaning that runs through all or most of the pertinent data
2. One in the minority that carries heavy emotional or factual impact (1991, 150)

Developing themes begins with the process of grouping data into patterns. Patterns are "recurring ideas, themes, perspectives, and descriptions that depict the social world you are studying" (Rossman and Rallis 1998, 179). One approach is to list some procedures that you can use as you begin to group data into patterns.

1. Read through and familiarize yourself with all your data. This can be a very tedious process but is necessary for you to get a complete understanding of what you have collected at your field site.

2. Keep a running commentary on any ideas that come to mind and record these as memos in your journal.
3. Review an interview, journal recording, or field note and look for the underlying meaning of what you are reading. Again, make notes.
4. Organize your data by grouping them into an array of patterns.

Keep in mind that other people reading your data might code it differently and develop different themes from the ones you organized. This is to be expected since our own knowledge and experiences shape our interpretation of what we see in the data. What is important is that you be able to explain your reasoning for what you organized and the categories you created. You need to state clearly what rules of evidence you used to organize and interpret your data. This is why you have a codebook so that others can see clearly how you did your work and why you did what you did. Someone may not agree with your interpretations, but that does not make them wrong. Your work is your contribution to the project.

The categories you create to organize your data will often help you discover themes by highlighting some relation among them. If you are inexperienced in field research, we suggest that you develop your coding categories before you try to develop your themes. By doing this you are anchoring your findings in the data or field notes (Ely 1991, 151). It is crucial at this juncture to begin to understand how various patterns in your data relate to each other. It is also the time to reflect on the conceptual framework you devised, which should be guiding your data analysis.

Ultimately, seeing patterns in your observations will lead to developing themes. You are likely to develop far more themes than you can pursue in your project. How do you select those themes you want to explore in the confines of your field research? A strategy is to select those themes for which you have the most data, or those themes you believe are most important to the people in the field (Emerson, Fretz, and Shaw 1995, 157).

We return to the student who was studying occupational transition of refugees in the United States for his discussion of themes:

> *Through analysis of the data generated, I identified several salient themes that affect occupational transition, including emotional separation from loved ones and culture, the use of family and ethnic networks to find jobs, the need to work long hours, the need to seek more education, and perceptions about opportunity or the American Dream in the United States.*

He claims that these may not be the only themes related to occupational transition, but these were reoccurring themes in the data generated in his study.

Regardless of the strategy you use, you will probably need to reclarify this process over time. You need to include as many of the voices and perspectives in your study as possible. The ability to do this is one of the most challenging aspects of practicing sociology. *To suspend your own view of the social world and see the world through the eyes of others is crucial to understanding social life and social problems.*

REFLECTING

Now that you have developed themes that you want to explain, it would be useful to reflect on these before you develop your explanations. Reflection is a conscious, intentional activity of thinking about and connecting ideas and observations. It is a process that helps you bridge the university and the community to ensure that practicing sociology is an ongoing process. One way to encourage reflection is through your coursework. In your courses, you communicate with one another through talking. Through talking you relate your feelings, information, facts, and ideas. Here is an example of reflecting and why it is essential for critical thinking.

> Sometime ago, it occurred to me that we spend a considerable amount of time helping people to improve their reading and writing skills as students, but we do little or nothing to help them learn to talk more effectively. This has always seemed both curious and misguided to me since talking is clearly one of our primary means of communicating with one another. . . . Crescimanno (1991, 2)

Thus, learning to speak effectively is a crucial skill for reflecting upon what you have seen, read, and learned through other means. Participation in class discussion is essential for a reflective learning experience in your community-based learning program. This participation will take several forms: (1) discussion of the assignments and readings and applying these concepts to your community or organization assignment; (2) discussion of your observations from the fieldwork site, drawing or focusing on sociological concepts; (3) discussion of your written assignments; (4) discussion of ethical issues that arise from your community learning experience, such as who owns the data you generate when you are doing your research; and (5) discussion of book reviews that you share with your classmates. Discussion encourages the process of reflection and makes you think more critically about the data in the field site.

Interruption of the taken-for-granted world of the learner is at the heart of the critical thinking and reflecting process (Crescimanno 1991). There is sometimes a tendency to stay on the surface of the material and to deal with it superficially. You need to step further into the material. It is equally important for you to be able to write what you learn, to say what you know and do not know. Reflection is the necessary process for this learning.

Reflection involves participation by extending your thinking to various interpretations on what you have observed. It is the complexity of structural relations that develop out of reflection. If you are using a critical approach you will find alternative explanations from what you have believed all along or different from other theoretical approaches that you have learned. You return to your courses, review your notes, and reflect on how these are useful for you in interpreting your observations and field notes. Then you are prepared to challenge and question your taken-for-granted views and explanations of what is happening around you.

THEORIZING

After you have described, organized, and analyzed your data, developed themes and reflected upon your work, your next step is to develop some tentative explanations for what you have created. This process is theorizing. Theory is an important component of all research. When you do field research in the community or an organization, you will be using theory to create rather than discover knowledge. You will be moving back and forth between data analysis and explanation, drawing from your sociological knowledge including concepts and theories. You "continue to watch, ask, and listen. You become analytic and reflective during the data gathering process" (Rossman and Rallis 1998, 164).

You will be drawing on existing concepts and theories to help you develop explanations from your observations that move your study beyond the level of description. Description has limited application for you if you want to engage in social justice work. You need to have at least tentative explanations to give interested people as to what you found and why. We refer to this as theorizing. You are interested in connecting your observations and interpretations with broader sociological knowledge. To do this, you need to return to your purpose and focus.

For many of you this will be a new experience and may seem overwhelming. We encourage you to look at the process that is involved rather than the label. What you are seeking to do is to provide alternative explanations or arguments for why you created what you did. Again, some people will not agree with the alternatives you provide but if they can understand how you reached these arguments, then you are in a position to convince them that what you created is probably the best set of arguments. That is why you need to demonstrate how the interpretations you advance are grounded in your data. To do this you follow the processes we discussed previously: detailed describing, coding, organizing, analyzing, developing themes, and reflecting. All this is done with a rigorous and disciplined approach.

TELLING THEIR STORIES

Practicing sociology lends itself to many ways of presenting your findings other than the traditional research report or paper. However, careful attention is always paid to the essential components of doing research. In this section we identify a few alternatives for presenting your fieldwork. This may be your first experience with using a different format from the usual research paper.

There are many ways that you can present these fieldwork stories, and one of the most effective is through storytelling. Sherryl Kleinman (1999) cautions us to write ethnographic stories in such a way that we "show" what we learned rather than just "telling" a story. When you do this you are able to help the community understand social interaction, inequality, and power, rather than just a drama of personalities.

Your choices of what stories to tell will likely be guided by the community issues you are studying. There are many options and strategies you and some community members may want to do together. You may want to write a magazine article or a letter to the editor of a local newspaper. Another strategy may be to prepare a report for a local government agency, drawing on the local information available to you. You may decide to give several oral presentations or organize a roundtable discussion. Some of these strategies may be useful in service-learning advocacy. If you are working in a community with homeless children, a letter to the editor, based on your research findings, would be one example of using your research findings as a means of social advocacy. You might draw attention to poverty and how it affects children who, through no fault of their own, are homeless. Using the same example, a handbook that highlights various measures that can be used to help homeless children is also a means of social action and another way to present your research findings. You might want to focus a handbook on what children in general can do to help empower homeless children. Perhaps such a handbook would be useful for distribution in elementary schools. These examples suggest how important it is to define early on what you wish to study during your fieldwork; decisions made early in the process shape what you can do with your findings.

There are other ways to present the results of your fieldwork. Depending on such things as your writing abilities, technical skills, availability of presentation sites, and so on, how you present your research findings can be far-reaching. We encourage you to work with your professor and the community to find ways that are most exciting for you. Community members are likely to have valuable insights on how best to present the findings with the most value and impact. Furthermore, community members may have more resources for communicating the findings in a variety of formats. "Finally, preparing and presenting research findings is an empowering process that brings benefits of all kinds to students and community members alike" (Strand et al. 2003, 117–118).

In this section we review one way to tell a story that differs from writing a paper. We provide you with a brief review on how to prepare an ethnography.

WRITING A RESEARCH ETHNOGRAPHY

Writing an ethnography is difficult because it requires that you think and organize differently from writing a traditional term paper. Writing an ethnography may be a new experience for most of you so we suggest you start by writing your first ethnography in two parts. *Doing this encourages you to write and think during the entire community-based learning experience.* You need to start writing when you begin the process of finding a community-based learning program.

For the first part of your ethnography, we suggest you begin your writing immediately, describing and reflecting on the first half of your community-based learning experience. Sometimes people wait until they have to write a report to begin reflecting. We argue that this process should start immediately when you begin your research. You need to continue writing and reflecting during the entire community-based learning program. Here is a list of possible topics to include in the first part of your ethnography, which should be written not later than the middle of the semester:

1. Write an introduction, using a pseudo name for your community or organization, in which you briefly describe how and why you chose this community study or organization.

2. Describe the purposes of the community study, discuss what the community or organization does, the goals and mission and how these are carried out, the positions and roles that are part of the organization or community, and where it is located. Try to obtain a table of organization for the organization and discuss the responsibilities associated with the positions, and the levels of authority and hierarchy among them. If you are working on a community project and the above do not apply, describe the community and its members, and your role in the community.

3. Describe in detail your position and role in the community and/or organization, including your activities, tasks, and responsibilities. Did you participate in the selection of these tasks? Have these changed since you started?

4. Describe your learning experience to this point in the semester. What have you learned as a sociologist and as a fieldworker since you started? Discuss any problems or tensions you have experienced in completing your tasks or in working with others.

5. Critically evaluate your time as a fieldworker and as a sociologist in this organization or community. Explain how your coursework or other classes prepared you for this fieldwork. Explore how your classes could have better prepared you to gain a more in-depth sociological understanding of the community. Suggest some ways to improve your fieldwork experience. Has your fieldwork experience prepared you to contribute to social advocacy and social change in the community?

6. Reflect on what you have observed in the community. Have you started to notice patterns and/or issues in the organization or community that you could discuss as a sociologist? Try to use the concepts you have read in this guide and learned in your coursework to gain further understanding of a community or organization.

Now that you have completed part one of your critical evaluation of your fieldwork, you are ready to reflect about how you will analyze your observations and write your final ethnography. You should be thinking about alternative explanations for what you are observing in the community. Because you have written answers to the previously-listed topics, you will be prepared to evaluate and reflect on your fieldwork experience and to complete a sociological analysis of the community or organization in which you did your fieldwork.

Here are some guidelines that may be useful to you before you start writing the second phase of your ethnography. Remember, research is an iterative process, constantly weaving back and forth between action and reflection. If you have been diligent in keeping your journal, then you will enjoy this phase of your project since you will have been writing all along.

We suggest that you begin your final ethnography with a revised and updated version of the field report we discussed earlier. Write this as a narrative history, following the outline we used previously. As you revise this report, be sure to include any changes that happened during your fieldwork and how you perceived these during your experiences in the community. You do not need to include your sociological analysis in this narrative history.

In the second part of your ethnography, use sociological concepts and ideas to make sense of the observations you made in your fieldwork and any other relevant documents you may have collected. You are trying to tell a sociological "story" to the community or organization about your observations.

In addition, you may have to tell a different story to meet your academic requirements. As we mentioned earlier, your effort in the community or organization is to bridge the university and the community, as well as do action research in the community. In the previous section we discussed telling your story in the community or organization. Now we talk more formally in terms of meeting your academic requirements. Be sure to check with your professor for clear guidelines on what you are supposed to include. We suggest some ideas below.

1. Carefully study your data and read through your notes that you have coded for recurring patterns and themes. Note any of these patterns or themes that you could discuss sociologically.
2. Then apply sociological concepts to explain and make sense of some of the patterns of social life you observed. These concepts can be from any reading or sociology courses you have taken. Refer to your journal for the reading summaries that you created. Discuss with your classmates and others as many possible concepts as you think may be applied to your observations. At some point, you will want to return to your original research questions.
3. Now you are ready to write your analysis. After you have reflected on all of the sociological concepts and ideas that come to you, choose several to use in analyzing your organization or community. Apply those concepts that make the most sense for the "story" you want to tell and those that you have the best "evidence" (examples from your observations) to support. Try to make the concepts work together in some way to form a cohesive paper. Define your concepts clearly and cite them in your paper. Also, support the concepts with detailed examples drawn from your field notes or other sources.

When you submit your final paper, include the following topics in whatever order your faculty require: an abstract, introduction, background, purpose, research questions, methodology, methods, analysis and analysis summary, discussion, and conclusions.

Learning to write an ethnography may seem a formidable task. It would be useful to read some ethnographies in your field of interest before you start writing your own. If you are interested in criminology you will want to read the ethnography by Sudhir Venkatesh, *American Project: The Rise and Fall of a Modern Ghetto* (2000). He analyzes the life of the "community" of Robert Taylor Homes, a public housing complex completed in 1962, including an in-depth ethnographic analysis of the Black Kings street gang. For those of you interested in public policy and social justice, you might be interested in *Making Grey Gold, Narratives of Nursing Home Care* (1990) by Timothy Diamond. His curiosity about the work in nursing homes developed out of a meeting he had with two African-American women who were employed as nursing assistants. Diamond's ethnographic study was guided by "theoretical questions" he devised about how nursing homes worked. Based on his findings, Diamond highlights ways in which the "everyday life" in nursing homes might be changed.

USES OF YOUR RESEARCH

When learning research at the undergraduate level, you usually focus on techniques and procedures, as well as those skills that will get you employment at some later time. Less attention is usually given to helping you understand the practical relevance of your research. In general, our academic value system does not support teaching the potential use of research. Robert Lynd (1939), a sociologist, addressed this in the classic book, *Knowledge for What?* He raised the question of why the scholar-scientist is not concerned with the **practical relevance** of research. This is not the place to try and answer his question but we believe you must be encouraged to use your research skills in ways that support a commitment to social justice. In the following sections, we address how field research and ethnography can be useful in providing social service, social action, and social change.

SOCIAL SERVICE

When you do field research, you are studying and learning the culture of a particular group. You are learning the patterns of behavior, artifacts, and knowledge that people have learned or created. Many sociologists agree that every human society is culturally constituted. When you act as an ethnographer and field researcher, you participate, observe, and ask questions to discover the cultural meanings known to insiders. When you analyze your field notes, you are beginning the process of going beyond mere descriptions of behavior to discover the cultural meaning of that behavior and the things you see.

The next step in the process is to use the findings for some humanitarian gain. For example, Spradley (1980, 17) argues that ethnographers must consider the potential uses of their research. Ethnography for what? Are we going to study the culture of poverty or child abuse to build new theories only, or do we want to do something about the culture of poverty? Do we want to change the social arrangements in society that create and maintain growing poverty among children? You will want to reflect on these questions as you participate in a community-based learning program.

Most researchers will agree that our cultural descriptions can be used to oppress people or to set them free. Field research on poverty needs to address how to change an unjust system. We can synchronize the needs of people and the goals of ethnography by following the list at the top of the next page.

1. Consulting with informants to determine urgent research topics
2. Developing the area of "strategic research" (Spradley 1980)

With the first effort, the community can develop a research agenda to relate the urgent community issues to the topics of concern within social science. If this is done, then the needs of the informants will have equal weight with scientific interest in setting ethnographic priorities. Strategic research begins with an interest in human problems, instead of beginning projects from an interest in some particular culture or theoretical concerns. Human problems suggest needed changes and information needed to make these changes. Ethnography should be used for understanding the human species, and for serving the needs of humankind (Spradley 1980). For us, this means social action.

SOCIAL ACTION

Social action refers to an activity formed through social interaction. This action can be that of an individual or that of an institution such as the government, media, or family. Social action is embedded in two processes: human agency and social structure. Tensions exist between these two processes that generate phenomena such as poverty, gender violence, and racism.

In a successful community-based learning program, your research becomes the impetus for social action. An important aspect of a community-based learning program is the opportunity to use research findings to bring about changes in the social structure that created inequalities associated with poverty, violence, racism, and so on.

History shows that people have actively raised questions about conditions in their communities and have searched for knowledge to help themselves. Social advocates propose to help communities use this knowledge to transform it into ways of improving their lives through social action. Advocacy creates a new framework of political will to promote research as collective action in the struggle over power and resources (Sohng 1995). How to acquire and use knowledge in the pursuit of social action is essential for the empowerment of communities.

As we have discussed earlier in this chapter, a commitment to social justice is most likely to be accomplished through practicing sociology in the community with a critical thinking approach. Community members' involvement in all stages is more likely to result in empowerment than the use of other research strategies. This empowerment is necessary for changes to be made in the social structures that control and oppress communities and their members.

SOCIAL CHANGE

Practicing sociology implies that exploring human relations through systematic inquiry should lead to the pursuit of social justice and social change. This remains a controversial process in community-based learning programs and in sociology (Lewis 2004). Yet, sociology and community-based programs are well suited to each other.

Kerry Strand et al. (2003) state "The third and perhaps most important aim of critical pedagogy is social change, a principle central to community-based research as well" (132). We agree with them and other sociologists that education ought to be liberatory, especially the discipline of sociology. Furthermore, we, along with Young (1990), have argued against oppression and domination in the pursuit of social justice. Our perspective argues that critical thinking and reflection are essential to changing the many social injustices that exist in the United States, especially the conditions of poverty that continue among children.

Finally, like Strand et al. (2003, 132) we see the need for a new approach to the many social injustices that exist. This new approach would move our current commitment from a charity model to a social justice model that embraces social advocacy (Lewis 2004). When you are a social advocate, you are engaged in changing the structural and institutional practices that contribute to unjustified inequalities. This means you are working to empower people to make decisions that affect their life chances. Hopefully, it means you will continue to engage in social advocacy in the community during your lifetime.

CONCLUSION

In this chapter, we have focused on the excitement of a broad discovery approach to understanding social phenomena rather than a technique-oriented approach based in a logic of discovery. We see the research process as a craft, in which your competence is acquired by continuous practice and experience-based knowledge. Our commitment is to bring excitement to the process of doing fieldwork and field research, rather than training you to be fieldworkers. When you finish this guide, you will be able to understand what community researchers do, why they do it, and how they do it. You will have the basis for further developing your skills when you are ready. Finally, you will have the preparation to make a commitment to practicing sociology in the pursuit of social justice.

REFLECTIONS

I. PRACTICING YOUR SKILLS

We think you will find it helpful to practice using the data generating methods we have described in this chapter so that you feel more comfortable going into the field. The following exercises may seem simple and insignificant but, if you try them, you are likely to have a better appreciation of what you will be looking for in the field. It is important that you focus on generating detailed observations, sometimes unobtrusively. With the participant observation exercise, you do not need to tell anyone what you are doing.

A. Participant Observation

You have decided to be an **observer** only in an eating setting that you are familiar with and a time period when this place will be busy. This allows you plenty of behavior to observe. Also, you will be in a place where you have a good idea of where you can sit and observe unobtrusively while taking careful **detailed** notes of what you observe. Decide ahead of time how long you will observe. For example, select an activity such as the behavior of people in line waiting to get their food or orders in. Observe the norms of "line behavior." Do all students follow the same rules in terms of waiting for their turn; do some students push ahead in the line and thus break the tacit rules of line behavior; do students react differently to the variations in line behavior; do students talk to each other? Describe the diversity in gender, ethnicity, and age.

In addition, do a "mapping" scheme of the physical environment. For example, describe where the meals are served and describe the eating spaces. Are these areas open, crowded, or difficult to move around in? What types of decorations are on the walls? Repeat this observation period two times and compare your findings. Reflect on your experiences. Do you feel more comfortable when using the method of participant observation? Did you pick up more detail the second time you observed?

B. Interviewing

Choose an area of interest to you and select two persons who are knowledgeable in this area to interview. For example, you may want to interview two seniors in your major field to determine why they chose their major field of study, what their careers goals are, and what they plan to do after graduation. You can find the names of graduating seniors from your department office. Call or e-mail the persons you selected from the list and ask if they would be willing to talk with you for twenty minutes or so. Tell them why you are interested in talking with them and how you will protect their confidentiality. Take written notes instead of using a tape recorder. Develop an interview guide with two or three general questions so that the person is free to talk about whatever has shaped their decisions. Such verbs as describe, explain, discuss are general and will lead to lengthy conversations. Remember, the purpose is to listen and make brief notes that you can write up after the interview. Reflect on your behavior during and after each interview. Did you feel more confident in the second interview? Why or why not? Do you need more practice? What did you learn about your skills as an interviewer? Reflect on these two interviews to decide if you need further practice. Discuss these experiences in class.

C. Document Analysis

Many people, including college administrators, parents, and students consider crime on college campuses an important issue. In 1992, the Federal Campus Security Act, now the Cleary Act, mandated the public release of campus crime statistics. To the present, many schools fail to report.

According to the *Chronicle of Higher Education* (June 9, 2000), the number of incidents of crime on 481 campuses with more than 5,000 students have increased from 1997 to 1998. For example, forcible sex offenses increased from 1,114 to 1,240, an 11.3 percent increase in one year. Nonforcible sex offenses increased from 125 in 1997 to 159 in 1988, a 27.2 percent increase. Aggravated assault went from 2,205 to 2,267, an increase of 2.8 percent. Arson increased 16.9 percent in one year from 461 incidents to 539. Incidents of hate crimes went from 155 to 179, an increase of 15.5 percent.

Some incidents of crime decreased. Manslaughter, robbery, burglary, and motor-vehicle theft all decreased from 1997 to 1998. Of these, motor-vehicle thefts constitute the most incidents with 4,272 in 1997 and 4,160 in 1998.

As part of your analysis, determine what the data are. What do these data show? Try to explain the data, remembering that social life is complex and there are likely to be several explanations. Draw from your knowledge in previous classes, if you can. Try to be as exhaustive as possible in your search for explanations. Finally, analyze each of your explanations. Are these individual explanations for the data or are they structural explanations?

II. What Would You Change?

When you have completed your research project, it is always useful to go back and reflect on the process and your project. What did you learn? What helped you develop your ability to practice sociology? Were there any limitations on what you could do? In addition, it is extremely useful to discuss your project with others in class: Learning is a social experience. Think of the following questions when you do your evaluation.

1. When you are doing participant observation, there is a relationship between you and the researcher. Apply your critical reflection skills to make clear your biases and assumptions. Write down with illustrations how you did this.
2. Reflect on how you linked your observations and concepts. Describe the process.
3. Explain how you used your critical thinking to take into account conflicting explanations.

CHAPTER 6

Engaging in Social Justice

Practicing sociology in the community is one means of bridging the university and the community in the pursuit of social justice. In this chapter we examine how these links occur by returning to a more in-depth look at promoting social justice in the community. We focus on a persistent social issue in the United States: poverty in general, and poverty among children. We bring in the voices of children by looking at not-for-profit organizations whose mission is advocacy for children, for example the National Association of Child Advocates (NACA) and the Children's Defense Fund (CDF). Some of these organizations use data collected by federal and state governments, who have missions other than advocacy.

Children have few lobbying advocates to represent them in positions of power and public policy. According to Carol DeVita and Rachel Mosher-Williams in *Who Speaks for America's Children* (2001), "Without question, America's poorest children remain in desperate need of an effective voice to speak on their behalf" (xvii). Children need advocates since they are unable to influence the conditions for becoming empowered in the United States. They are unable to participate in, negotiate with, influence, control, or hold accountable institutions that affect their lives.

As a brief background, we begin by looking at the meanings of poverty in the United States and at who is poor. Next, we examine poverty among children and its related consequences. We explore how to empower children who remain oppressed and unable to make choices affecting their future. We finish with ideas on how you can make a difference and work as an advocate for social justice. To do this you must be curious and wonder about the conditions around you rather than just accepting things the way they are.

POVERTY IN THE UNITED STATES

In this section, we examine two socially constructed concepts: "poverty" and "poor." Remember these are concepts and not real entities. However, poverty is not just a description of poor people. It is a social relationship that exists within a social structure. How poor people carry out their lives is not simply a matter of underachievement or lack of money. It is based on how society is organized in ways that keep the underclass under and the working poor, poor. Like other social conditions, there is a long history of how these social relationships became a central part of our lives. After a brief review of these concepts, we examine some statistics on poverty in the United States.

If you are going to practice sociology in the pursuit of social justice you need to read more about persistent social issues in the United States, including poverty. You need to apply critical thinking and reflection to understand this and other continuing problems. For example, you need the curiosity to learn more about how poverty is measured and if different measures would be more likely to address the limitations of how poverty is calculated.

Some policymakers argue that the official poverty rate is overestimated because only annual cash income is counted in determining whether a family is poor. They argue that the current rate does not include benefits from noncash programs such as food stamps, medical care, and housing benefits. If it did, then the poverty rate would be lower. Others argue that the current measure of the poverty rate is useful because it remains consistent over time, it adjusts for need, and at least initially it was based on some real measure of adequate income level for basic survival.

There are other critics of how poverty is measured who argue that the poverty rate would be higher if the income and payroll taxes were subtracted from gross family income to calculate the net family resources available to pay shelter, food, and clothing. There is a group of policymakers and academicians who represent themselves as The Working Group on Revising the Poverty Measure. If you are interested in the arguments on this measure you can find their letter to the director of the Office of Management and Budget, Census Bureau, at http://www.ssc.wisc.edu/irp/povmeas/povlet.htm. How the poverty rate is measured is a political issue, and you will be hearing more about this in the near future.

How poverty is measured has political and social policy consequences. Political consequences can be seen in how effective the administrations are in reducing poverty during their political reign. Politicians, to some extent, are likely to be judged in terms of what the poverty rate is and how this compares with past performances. The measurement of poverty has consequences for social policy and many other federal and federal-state programs. There are many federal and state programs that provide cash or in-kind aid to low-income persons, for example food stamps, that are directly linked to official poverty guidelines.

As you read this section on meanings of poverty and poor, consider the following questions:

1. Who is poor in America? How do you know this?
2. Do you know how poverty is measured? Who measures poverty?
3. Is poverty different for different groups in the United States?

4. What are some social policy and political consequences of our current poverty measure?
5. What does being poor mean to you? What factors or persons have influenced how you think of being poor and in poverty?
6. What does being poor mean to those people who are counted as poor? Do you think there is a common ground between what people who are poor are actually saying and what scholars and officials are saying about poor people?

Using a critical thinking approach to reflect on these questions will lead you to a better understanding of the issue of poverty in America and the data behind these findings.

MEANINGS OF "POVERTY" AND "POOR"

The terms **poverty** and **poor** are often confused with each other and often used synonymously. When we talk about being poor we are describing a condition. When we talk about poverty we are describing a social system in which most of the poor have lower-level jobs that are essential to the viability of our society, for example, janitors and berry pickers. J. Gordon and Mary N. Chamberlin, in *First Report: Program on Understanding Poverty* (2000), suggest that the confusion between the terms lies to a great extent in the federal government's "poverty line" concept. The argument is "that families with incomes below the poverty line are 'in poverty,' while those with incomes above the line are no longer poor for they are 'out of poverty'" (Chamberlin and Chamberlin 2000, 8). They continue, "Were that the case, it would mean that in 1993 a family of four with an income of $14,500 was no longer poor in a country with a per capita income, then, of $18,841" (Chamberlin and Chamberlin 2000, 8).

Being "poor" is a relative term. Bishop Leibrecht, National Conference of Catholic Bishops, reports that in 1999, some 11.8 percent of the total U.S. population, or 32.3 million people, found themselves living in poverty—defined as those whose annual cash income is less than that determined by the federal government as necessary for minimal nutritional subsistence and basic living costs (Leibrecht 2001). The poverty threshold in 1999 was $17,184 for a family of four. We know, however, that there were many people who were "poor" in 1999 who earned more than the limits of the poverty threshold but were not paid a living wage. These are the working poor who constitute a large number in the United States today. According to the Economic Policy Institute (2001), 29 percent of working families in the United States with one to three children under age twelve do not earn enough income to afford basic necessities like food, housing, health care, and childcare. The average poverty threshold for a family of four in 2001 was $18,100 in annual income. The Catholic Campaign for Human Development (CCHD) found in its study that most Americans believe it takes close to $35,000 annually to adequately house, clothe, and feed a family of four (2002). We turn now to a historical view on how the federal government and academicians have defined poverty in America.

Defining Poverty

The federal government began defining poverty in 1961 (Sullins 2001). Prior to this date, the states had individual, sometimes inconsistent, estimates of poverty. The federal government established the poverty rate that measures the proportion of a population whose cash income is below a certain amount. The process, used by the federal government to develop poverty thresholds, began with analysts at the

Social Security Administration using the U.S. Department of Agriculture's least expensive plan for nutritional subsistence, called the "Economy Food Plan." The amount from this plan was multiplied by three to allow for expenses other than food. The resulting amount was multiplied by the number of persons in a family to produce a sliding threshold of poverty based on family size. Each year this amount is indexed to increasing food costs to form the official definition of poverty. Some argue that this threshold, or line, has little to do with what it costs to live or with what it means to be "poor" to most people (Chamberlin and Chamberlin 2000, 8).

The poverty line is an arbitrary line and contributes to confusion and further detriment to poor people. What being poor means to many people may or may not be connected to the poverty line as determined in these studies.

> A second confusion [between poverty and being poor] has to do with the common assumption that the words "poor" and "poverty" are simply economic questions. While poverty refers to economic realities, it like all other economic ideas, expresses cultural values and relationships. It is produced and perpetuated by the choices and beliefs of those who take our inherited institutional structures and practices for granted as acceptable cultural norms. (Chamberlin and Chamberlin 2000, 8–9)

There are many meanings of being poor, depending on which group in our society defines this concept. A survey by CCHD, *Poor Americans Speak Out About Poverty* provided a special look into the attitudes of poor Americans about the state of poverty in our country (2002). This study used a survey of people who are poor and who were part of community-based, self-help organizations across the country that are initiated and led by low-income individuals. The goal of the survey was to learn how poor people see poverty today and what solutions they feel would help them get out of poverty. We list a few of the findings from this study.

1. What it means to be poor in the United States was described as not having a home or adequate housing, and not enough money to meet basic needs.
2. Being poor in the United States is depressing, degrading, being looked down on, ignored, or feeling hopeless, lonely, and powerless.
3. When asked about the biggest problem facing society in the United States today, those surveyed named unemployment, discrimination, and poverty as the three top concerns. Next were education, affordable housing, health care, crime, and drug/alcohol addiction.
4. Most persons in the survey cited education as a key cause of poverty. Lack of access to education, lack of a living wage or employment opportunities, unjust social policies were also cited as causes of poverty.
5. When asked "What is the best way to help permanently put an end to poverty," they answered: having more community-based organizations that help the poor directly (38 percent); providing government assistance to the poor (19 percent); and giving money to organizations that help the poor (17 percent). (CCHD 2002)

You have read about the concepts, beliefs, culture, ideology, norms, values, empowerment, and oppression in many places in this guide. You have learned how to apply these concepts to social issues. This can help you analyze why being poor means something different than being in poverty. In the text that follows we list a few data sources on poverty that provide a brief glimpse of a persistent problem in America.

SELECTED STATISTICS ON POVERTY IN THE UNITED STATES

State and federal agencies keep statistics on poverty and revise these every few years. The U.S. Census Bureau collects income data on several major national surveys:

1. Annual Demographic Supplement to the March Current Population Survey (CPS)
2. Survey of Income and Program Participation (SIPP)
3. Census 2000 long form
4. Census 2000 Supplementary Survey (C2SS), and the 2001 and 2002 Supplementary Surveys
5. American Community Survey (ACS)

Each of these surveys differs from the others in length and detail of the question-naire, how the data were collected and processed, and thus in the income and pover-ty estimates produced. Remember, interpretation is a part of how these data were collected and processed. You will sometimes see different estimates depending upon the source you read. Be aware that these are estimates and not absolute truths. We draw from the U.S. Census Bureau (2002) reports for this review: "Poverty in the United States: 2001," and "Money Income in the United States: 2001." These are available on-line at http://www.ssc.wisc.edu/irp/faqs3.htm and http://www.policyalmanac.org/social_welfare/archive/poverty_statistics2001.

Selected Findings on Poverty

1. In 2001, about 1.3 million more people were poor than in 2000—32.9 million versus 31.6 million. The poverty rate had been falling the pre-vious four consecutive years.
2. In 2001, the number of poor families increased from 6.4 million in 2000 (8.7 percent of all families) to 6.8 million (9.2 percent).
3. Only non-Hispanic whites (up 905,000 to 15.3 million), and Hispanics (up 250,000 to 8.0 million) saw an increase in the number of poor.
4. Increases in poverty were concentrated in metropolitan areas (partic-ularly outside central cities in the suburbs) and in the South. The South was the only region to have an increase in its poverty rate from 2000 to 2001. Its rate of 13.5 percent was the highest among all regions.
5. The average "poverty" threshold for a family of four in 2001 was $18,100 in annual income; compared with $14,128 for a family of three; $11,569 for a family of two; and $9,039 for unrelated individuals.

Selected Findings on Income

1. Median household income declined 2.2 percent in real terms from its 2000 level to $42,228 in 2001.
2. The real median earnings of women age fifteen and older who worked full time, year-round increased for the fifth consecutive year, rising to $29,215, a 3.5 percent increase between 2000 and 2001.

3. The share of income going to the poorest fifth of households declined, from 3.6 percent to 3.5 percent. Almost all the measures examined in the report show inequality to be above its 1999 and earlier levels.

Another study of income during the 1990s shows that the gap between rich and poor throughout the country had inched wider during the 1990s. For example, in Washington, D.C., the average income of families in the wealthiest fifth of the population, once adjusted for inflation, grew to twenty-four times the average in the bottom fifth, up from eighteen times (Scott 2001). Andrew Beveridge, a sociologist who conducted the study, found there is a worsening of income inequality. Furthermore, he noted a decline in the average income of families in the middle (Scott 2001).

Critical Thinking and Statistics

Researchers use statistics for many purposes, often to make a persuasive case concerning a social issue or problem. Many people find statistics to be convincing because we have been told that numbers are real, objective cases of something, and thus carry legitimate authority. This is especially likely when the statistics are collected by government authorities. In this case, statistics may have rhetorical value and are not questioned by many researchers.

You should apply your critical thinking when you read statistics even though you may have confidence in the sources. Some questions you might ask are as follows: What sources of bias and error can be found in these numbers? What do you know about how the populations and samples were identified and selected? What questions were asked and how were the categories used in the questionnaire selected and by whom? What do you know about the agency that collected the data and analyzed it? What motives might the agency involved have for doing the study? We caution you to reflect on these questions when you read and interpret the above statistics. Write down your answers to these questions and put them in your journal for later review.

Now that you have read these statistics, reflect on how to make sense of them. Can you see any social issues in these findings? Did these statistics surprise you? If not, why do you think poverty conditions continue for so many Americans and continue to grow? If you were surprised by these findings, write down how you came up with these tentative explanations. What do these findings mean to you? What connections do you make to these findings? How do you evaluate these findings based on what you learned in Chapter 2? For example, what ideologies support the persistence of poverty in America? Do you believe the American credo that if you work hard you will be able to achieve what you want? Do you blame the poor for being poor? What values support the persistence of poverty in America?

We continue with some statistics on poverty among children in the United States. Before you read this section, write down any ideas that you have formed about how poverty affects children. Have you observed poverty conditions among children as you move around in your daily activities or in the communities in which you have lived? Have you read about poverty among children in the newspapers or heard about this on the daily news reports? Perhaps you have had little exposure to this issue, and the statistics described in the text that follows may be a surprise to you. There are several questions that one can think of. Are children worse off now than twenty to thirty years ago? Or are they better off in this twenty-first century? We look at a few sources to answer these questions.

POVERTY AMONG CHILDREN

There are many sources of data for studying poverty among children. We provide you with several of these and with additional references for you to explore poverty among children if you are interested. Next, we list some statistical findings from several agencies for you to consider and to reflect on.

INFORMATION SOURCES FOR POVERTY AMONG CHILDREN

There are several not-for-profit organizations that analyze data from the Census Bureau to write separate reports on particular issues. In addition, some of these organizations collect information on special topics. For example: National Center for Children in Poverty (NCCP), The Children's Defense Fund, CATO Institute, Brookings Institution: Center on Urban and Metropolitan Policy, and Coalition on Human Needs.

At least one federal government agency has children as part of its mission: U.S. Department of Health and Human Services, Administration for Children and Families (ACF). Finally, you will find coverage of issues related to social welfare and children by accessing http://www.yahoo.com: homelessness, poverty news, child welfare, disabilities, and the disabled. But whatever sources you access, one fact remains constant in all of the findings available to us: Child poverty rates continue to surpass those of working-age adults and the elderly. Poor children lag behind other children in terms of health, are more likely to do worse in school, become teen parents, and experience poverty as adults. However, it is important to point out that there is great variation among poor children in terms of their schooling, pregnancies, poverty as adults, and other aspects of life.

SELECTED FINDINGS ON POVERTY AMONG CHILDREN

We review a few findings on poverty among children and ask you to think about what you expect to read, or some other reaction you have to these statistics. Before you read these, write down what you know about children in poverty. Compare this with your reactions after you finish reading the findings. Discuss your reactions with your classmates to learn if there is a shared knowledge base on what myths have been accepted about children who are poor. Have you ever seen or heard about poor children sleeping in shelters in your community, or sleeping on your streets? If so, what was your reaction? Do you blame the children for being poor, do you blame the government, or do you blame the parents, if they have parents? What other tentative ideas do you have to explain children's poverty?

There are several not-for-profit organizations dedicated to improving the conditions of children in the United States. We review findings from two of these: National Center for Children in Poverty (NCCP), Columbia University. This study, *Wake Up America* (NCCP 2003b), tracked poverty rates for children under age six from 1975 to 1994: http://www.nccp.org/ycpf_03.html, May 14, 2003.

The study reports the following:

1. The young child poverty rate has grown to include one in four young children and that nearly 50 percent of American young children are near poverty or below.
2. The rate of young children in extreme poverty (with incomes below 50 percent of the poverty line) doubled from 6 to 12 percent.

3. The young child poverty rate grew twice as fast for whites (38 percent) as for blacks (19 percent).

4. Most poor children live in **working families** [bold in report] contrary to the commonly held belief that a family job will keep children out of poverty. In 1994, 62 percent of poor young children lived with at least one parent or relative who worked part or full time.

A second source of data on children comes from Child Trends, founded in 1979. This is an independent, nonpartisan research center dedicated to improving the lives of children and their families by conducting research and providing science-based information to the public and decision makers (Child Trends 2003). They report that between 1995 and 2000, the percentage of poor children living in working poor families rose steadily from 32 percent to 43 percent, before falling to 40 percent in 2001 (Child Trends 2003). Among poor children, those in married-couple families are more likely to qualify as working poor than those in single-mother families (60 percent versus 33 percent).

When you reflect on these statistics, do you think that giving working parents additional income would make conditions any better for children? Can you think of ways that you could explore this question by talking with people in the community? When we reviewed the literature we found an organization that had written a report on this issue: Boosting Income for Working Parents Pays Off for Children, http://www.mdrc.org. This study by MDRC, a non-profit, nonpartisan social policy research organization, suggests that cuts in financial incentives for low-income workers by budget-strapped state governments may have far-reaching consequences for vulnerable children and their families. Many of the concerns of the "near poor" low-income families overlap with those of the poor, such as the need for well-paying jobs and access to affordable quality child care and health care.

An update by the NCCP in March 2003 reveals the following profile of low-income children in the United States. The U.S. child poverty rate is substantially higher—often two to three times higher—than that of most other major Western industrialized nations. Children in America are almost twice as likely to live in poverty than Americans in any other age groups (NCCP 2003a). Thirty-eight percent of American children (27 million children) live in low-income families (42 percent of U.S. children under age six—almost 10 million children), http://www.nccp. org/ycpf_03.html. We asked the question earlier whether children are worse off today than previously. For example, children who are homeless are often not able to attend school because they lack vaccination records and addresses or telephone numbers where they can be located. The findings to date show that, using the current official measure of poverty, child poverty rates continue to surpass those of other age groups. Review these statistics and write in your journal at least three paragraphs on the ones that you were most unaware of or that amazed you the most.

WHY STUDY POVERTY AMONG CHILDREN?

Why is it important to study poverty among children? Why are so many children in poverty amidst all the wealth and prosperity in our country? One reason to advocate for improving the conditions for children is the known consequences of the effects of poverty among children. The National Center for Children in Poverty (NCCP) argues that reducing child poverty is a smart investment because fewer children in poverty will result in the following:

1. More children entering school ready to learn
2. More successful schools and fewer school dropouts

3. Better child health and less strain on hospitals and public health systems
4. Less stress on the juvenile justice system
5. Less child hunger and malnutrition, and other important advances (NCCP, March 2003a)

Throughout this guide we have introduced you to the idea of social justice. In large part we draw on the work of Young (1990) who argues that social justice, or more particularly injustice, is part of everyday life because it is embedded in our institutions and social systems. As such, we all consciously or unconsciously participate in an unjust society where many individuals and groups are unable to live life according to their own choosing.

This conceptualization is productive for understanding the complexities of social life and preparing you to take on an advocacy role at your learning site. A review of the previous chapters should point out to you that practicing sociology means developing and using a "critical consciousness." This consciousness allows you to see social problems as public issues and as part of the social arrangements in society. Once aware of these public issues, a pursuit of social justice implies taking action to change these oppressive structures. In the next section we draw your attention to structural arrangements in society that help create and maintain the oppression of children and suggest how these might be changed.

EMPOWERING CHILDREN

There are many who would argue that it is not possible to empower children in this very complex society in which we live. If it were possible, how would you do this? One way is to advocate for children. The Children's Defense Fund (CDF), founded in 1968 by Marian Wright Edelman, is probably the most well-known child advocacy organization in the country. Another is to provide a way for children to speak for themselves. For example, *Foster Care Youth United* begun in 1993, is a bimonthly magazine written by and for young people in foster care. Another way is to ensure these children have a safe space where they are protected from further harm and that their daily needs are met.

Children need to be empowered to participate in and shape community programs that will reduce their oppression. It is clear from the above findings on poverty that the injustices that children experience in the United States need to be changed. But one question remains: How do you empower children who are poor so that they can speak for themselves and make decisions that affect their lives? There is no united voice for children or for hearing the voices of children. Who speaks for children in Congress? Children do not vote. Empowering children is a political issue. Other questions to reflect on regarding how to empower children are discussed in the text that follows.

1. WHO SPEAKS FOR CHILDREN?

There are many advocacy organizations that speak for children on a variety of issues in a variety of ways. Their activities include lobbying in support of legislative action, public policy research and its dissemination to influence public opinion and policymakers, advertising campaigns to educate the public, and efforts to mobilize citizens to vote for specific candidates (DeVita and Mosher-Williams 2001, xiii–xiv).

While there are many agencies speaking for children, there are some constraints that limit their effectiveness. These are identified in *Who Speaks for America's Children? The Role of Child Advocates in Public Policy*, edited by Carol DeVita and Rachel Mosher-Williams (2001). We cite a few of their conclusions that are significant in promoting social justice for children in the future:

1. There is no consensus on the central issues facing children.
2. There is little agreement on the long-term value of community organizing or on the most successful strategies that child advocacy organizations should consider.
3. There is almost no agreement about whether child advocacy organizations should focus their efforts at the national, state, or local level, or about the implications of pursuing one or more of these approaches. (2001, xvii)

When you reflect on these findings, what comes to mind first? Using a sociological approach, what do you think needs to happen to bring about agreement on some of the issues above so that children's voices can be heard?

2. How Do We Protect and Improve Public Education?

Some people believe that educating children who are poor and homeless is another way to empower them. In Phoenix, Arizona, they have approached this problem by establishing the Thomas J. Pappas Elementary School for homeless children (Morrison 2001). Eleven years old, it is the largest and most developed school for homeless children, supported and partially funded by the state and by community donations. Volunteers mentor the children and help the teachers or work in other capacities. State-mandated curriculum is required. A school bus travels to find the children and bring them to school where they are fed, provided clothes as needed, and sometimes provided with medicines. But more importantly, this school provides a safe haven for children who are constantly on the go, never knowing where they might be from night to night.

The idea of setting up separate schools for homeless children has many critics, as well as supporters. Critics argue that these schools violate the McKinney Act by creating separate facilities for homeless students rather than integrating them into existing schools. The argument is that such programs are misusing federal funds and not making efficient use of government money. According to these critics, it would be better to put the children into regular public schools and spend the federal dollars on services to help them with tutoring and textbooks (Morrison 2001).

Many people support having separate schools for homeless children such as the Pappas School. They argue that children who are homeless need to have a place they feel safe, where they are protected, and have the necessary essentials of food and clothing so that they can benefit from an educational experience. The school is intended to be a transitional place where children can continue their education while their parents find stable addresses and jobs (Morrison 2001).

3. How Can We Hear Children's Voices?

When we put this question to many of our friends and colleagues, they answered: You have to listen to children's voices and the voices of the poor; you need to educate children so they can help themselves; and you have to provide a safe place for children to live and grow into adults. We asked ourselves, who is listening to children? We learned that many organizations speak for children but do not necessarily listen to children. Ernest Kurtz and Katherine Ketcham in *The Spirituality of Imperfection* discuss listening by referring to William James, who stated, "[T]o *listen* to others in such a way that we are willing to surrender our own worldview. . . . What happens first, in any 'community,' is that those who would participate in it *listen*" (2002, 94). The voices of children are not heard by many, as good intentioned people continue to do "for" children instead of doing "with" them.

4. How Does the Criminal Justice System Support Children?

The criminal justice system is large and complex, depending upon how you define it. To answer this question you need to have an understanding of how that system works, which we do not provide you in this discussion. We provide you with an example of one aspect of this system that protects children: the National Association of Counsel for Children (NACC). This association includes in its mission the empowering of children by ensuring that courts hear and consider the views of children in proceedings that affect children's lives. NACC attorneys work to ensure that children's views are heard in legal proceedings. NACC also supports programs that include the work of volunteers to represent children. One example is the Volunteer Court Appointed Special Advocates (CASA) program, which is in place in many states. CASA advocates are everyday people who are appointed by judges to advocate for the best interests of abused and neglected children. A CASA volunteer works with each child until he or she is placed into a safe, permanent, and nurturing home. National CASA supports a nationwide network of CASA programs that train and support CASA volunteers (http://www.nationalcasa.org).

We have given you a few ideas on how to explore the large issue of how to empower children. There are many more, for example, how do welfare laws affect children's empowerment; how does the availability of health care affect children's empowerment? There are many areas in which your curiosity should lead you to understand why children lack empowerment and how this contributes to the social injustices that these children experience.

As sociologists, we have argued in this guide that looking at individual characteristics cannot provide an understanding of why some groups in society are poor, especially children. Nor can a focus on individual characteristics change structural arrangements in society that create social problems, such as poverty among children and homelessness. More than 550,000 children live in foster care in the United States. The courts remove them from their homes when it is determined that they have been abused or neglected by parents. Often the source of neglect is family poverty.

Becoming a Social Advocate

If you decide to become an advocate for social justice as part of your community-based learning program, your critical thinking will enable you to move beyond short-term answers to bring about meaningful solutions. We give you some successful examples of how students have participated and made a difference in some communities. Part of their success is based in paying attention to four strategies that will be important to you.

1. Be sure your group or organization has done some groundwork, including researching and educating yourselves on the issue.
2. Identify key people and institutions you are aiming to influence.
3. Set clear, focused, and realistic goals and objectives.
4. Create strategic alliances (*Just Add Consciousness: A Guide to Social Activism* 2003). This publication represents the efforts of three organizations: Oxfam America, Campus Outreach Opportunity League (COOL), and Bread for the World. (http://oxfamamerica.org)

Part of educating yourself on the issue is to identify organizations in which students have supported issues that you are concerned about. For example, if you are interested in hunger, you might use the Internet to learn what, if anything, students have done in this area (Shiveley and VanFossen 2001). If you do, you will find the National Student Campaign Against Hunger (http://www.nscabb.org). You would also find students at Mt. Holyoke College generating political will to support their issues. Students at Mt. Holyoke College in Massachusetts visited their representative to seek support for proposed legislation and to become a co-sponsor on hunger fighting legislation. Where there are many co-sponsors for a piece of legislation it is likely to attract more attention to gain support. In this instance the students were significant in pushing legislation forward to help families have food and move toward ending hunger.

The Foundation for Jewish Campus Life (Hillel) provides more ideas on how to understand the root causes of issues and educate activists and the public (http://www.hillel.org/hillel/newhille.nsf). They generated a list of ABCs of Advocacy. In this list they encourage you to find your niche on your campus and in your community, find your cause, and find time. They add another strategy for you to follow: Listen! What issues excite students on your campus? Lobby for these issues. An important strategy they include is to partner with other campus and community-based organizations. Such alliances should be made after careful study to ensure your issues are addressed. This is part of the strategy of educating yourself as to what other organizations may be pursuing your interests.

As you read this guide, you see that we take a critical approach to understanding everyday life in the United States. This means we are trying to prepare you to question existing social arrangements in your community. Why are things the way they are? What can be done to change injustices? One way to start is by analyzing the way society is structured, rather than focusing on individual characteristics. The concepts of oppression and domination are grounded in a critical approach to examining social life. Through their application, you can uncover and help to make sense of social arrangements in this society that make it difficult for many people to live lives of their own choosing. Another way is to become an advocate for social justice. We hope you do this as part of your community-based learning program. If you want to learn more about how you can become an advocate, contact The Advocacy Institute at their e-mail: info@advocacy.org.

CONCLUSION

We wrote this guide to share with you our commitment to practicing sociology in the community in the pursuit of social justice. Hopefully, you have learned there is much work ahead of you. One area in which much needs to be done is the alleviation of poverty that surrounds all of us. People in power will continue to oppress and dominate poor people. Poverty will continue to exist and grow as a local and global problem.

A critical sociological approach requires you to use a structural approach to social issues, moving away from individual explanations for social phenomena with the use of systematic research. In so doing, you are well prepared not only to identify social problems that exist, but also to challenge existing social structures. Sam Marullo writes of these opportunities in the context of challenging sociologists who teach.

> It is up to sociologists to fulfill the role of teaching students how to undertake critical structural analysis. . . . Service-learning can be a vehicle for creating generations of students who can understand and appreciate the complexity of current social problems. . . . If we fulfill well our role as teachers, we will have produced adults who have good conceptual, analytical, and cognitive skills . . . who have clarified their values and develop their social skills in the crucible of real-life applications, who are committed and active citizens, and who are committed activists for social justice. (1999, 22)

It is your challenge to work with communities to reduce the causes and consequences of poverty and any other social injustices. It means that you are part of trying to alleviate these oppressive conditions. It means you begin by questioning the existing social arrangements in this society that make it difficult for people to live lives of their own choosing. It means, in the words of Peter Dreier (June 16, 2001), who spoke at the commencement address to sociology graduates at the University of Oregon,

> No matter what career you pursue, you have choices about how you will live your lives. As citizens, you can sit on the sidelines and merely be involved in your society. Or you can decide to become really *committed* to making this a better world.

We share with you a thoughtful word from a sociologist who is committed to making this a better world:

> What sociologists can offer the world has the potential to keep divine love alive. It is still a graceless world, and it may get worse before it gets better. We can't be part of what kills the human spirit. Sociology serves the social world, not the other way around. . . . We do sociology for love of the world. (Gaines 1998, 457)

We believe that there are means of changing the many injustices that people experience in this society. Practicing sociology in the pursuit of social justice is one of them. Professor Walda Katz-Fishman reinforced the focus of this guide when she said in her interview in Chapter 1: "We all need to reflect: coming back to our lived experiences, and thinking of what part we all can play in building today's movement for global justice and equality."

REFLECTIONS

I. SELF-EVALUATION

For your last reflection exercise, we ask you to return to the questions in the Reflections section in Chapter 1.

Review each question and review your answers to those questions. Now reflect on your answers. Would you write the same answers today?

1. Have your views changed or remained the same as to what you care about the most, the least? Explain your answers.

2. In your own words, write the meaning of critical thinking, critical reflection, and critical sociological approach. Use different examples to illustrate from those you used in Chapter 1.

3. What is the value to you of social advocacy? Did you have an opportunity to engage in advocacy during your community-based learning program? Are you interested in doing advocacy work at a later time?

4. Do you think you should work for social justice? Explain.

Bibliography

American Sociological Association. 1995. *Careers in Sociology.* 4th ed. Washington, D.C.

American Sociological Association. 1997. *Ethical Standards of the American Sociological Association Sections 1-11-08.* Washington, D.C.

Anderson, E. 1990. *Streetwise: Race, Class, and Change in an Urban Community.* Chicago, IL: University of Chicago Press.

Anderson, E. 2000. *Code of the Street: Decency, Violence, and the Moral Life of the Inner City.* New York: W. W. Norton & Company.

Baird, B. 1996. *The Internship, Practicum, and Field Placement Handbook: A Guide for the Helping Professions.* Upper Saddle River, NJ: Prentice Hall.

Baker, P., L. Anderson, and D. Dorn. 1993. *Social Problems: A Critical Thinking Approach.* Belmont, CA: Wadsworth Publishing Company.

Bean, J. 1996. *Engaging Ideas: The Professor's Guide to Integrating Writing: Critical Thinking, and Active Learning in the Classroom.* San Francisco, CA: Jossey-Bass.

Beeghley, L. 1997. "Demystifying Theory: How the Theories of Georg Simmel (and Others) Help Us to Make Sense of Modern Life." Pp. 267–273 in *The Student's Companion to Sociology,* edited by Jon Gubbay, Chris Middleton, and Chet Ballard. Oxford, UK: Blackwell Publishers.

Berg, B. 2001. *Qualitative Research Methods for the Social Sciences.* 4th ed. Boston, MA: Allyn and Bacon.

Berger, P., and T. Luckmann. 1966. *The Social Construction of Reality.* Garden City, NY: Doubleday.

Blanke, G. 1998. *In My Wildest Dreams.* New York: Simon & Schuster.

Bradley, H. 1997. "Social Divisions." Pp. 142–151 in *The Student's Companion to Sociology,* edited by Jon Gubbay, Chris Middleton, and Chet Ballard. Oxford, UK: Blackwell Publishers.

Bureau of Justice Statistics and The Sentencing Project. April, 2001. "Facts about Prisons and Prisoners." Washington, D.C. [On-line]. Available: http://www.sentencingproject.org/brief/facts-pp.pdf (July 1, 2002).

Cassell, C., and G. Symon. 1994. *Qualitative Methods in Organizational Research: A Practical Guide.* Thousand Oaks, CA: Sage.

Catholic Campaign for Human Development. 2003. "January Is Poverty in America Awareness Month: New Media Campaign Puts a Human Face on Poverty." [On-line]. Available: http://www.usccb.org/cchd/povertyusa/pressrel/paamnew.htm (May 25, 2003).

Catholic Campaign for Human Development. 2002. *Poor Americans Speak Out about Poverty.* [On-line]. Available: http://www.usccb.org/cchd/povertyusa/pulserel.htm (May 25, 2003).

Chamberlin, J. G., and M. N. Chamberlin. 2000. *First Report: Program on Understanding Poverty.* Greensboro, NC: Poverty Coalition, Inc.

Charon, J. 2001. *Ten Questions: A Sociological Perspective.* 4th ed. Belmont, CA: Wadsworth Publishing Co.

Chesler, M. 1993. "Community Service-Learning as Innovation in the University." [On-line]. Available: http://www.umich.edu/~ocsl/Proj_Community/coord/chesler1.html (March 12, 2004).

Child Trends. 2003. "Percent of Poor Children Living with Working Poor Drops." [Online]. Available: http://www.childtrends.org/n_WorkingParents.asp (June 4, 2003).

Chizeck, S. 1999. "Developing and Gaining Acceptance on Campus for an Internship Program." Pp. 38–47 in *The Internship Handbook: Development and Administration of Internship Programs in Sociology,* edited by Richard Salem. Washington, D.C.: American Sociological Association.

Chronicle of Higher Education. 2000. "Students: A Look at Campus Crime," June 9. [On-line]. Available: http://chronicle.com/free/v46/i40/40a04901.htm#1year (March 13, 2001).

Chubinski, S. 1996. "Creative Critical-Thinking Strategies." *Nurse Educator* 21: 23–27.

Cohen, A. 1992. *The Symbolic Construction of Community.* New York: Routledge.

Collins, R. 1998. "The Sociological Eye and Its Blinders." *Contemporary Sociology* 27: 2–7.

Colorado State University. 1997–2003. "Benefits of Reflection." [On-line]. Available: http://writing.colostate.edu/references/teaching/service_learning/refben.cfm.

Cooper, M. 1997. "Reflection: Getting Learning Out of Serving." [On-line]. Available: http://www.selu.edu/Academics/Faculty/dlongman/servreflect.html (March 12, 2004).

Cottle, S. 1997. "Society as Text: Documents, Artifacts and Social Practices." Pp. 282–289 in *The Student's Companion to Sociology,* edited by Jon Gubbay, Chris Middleton, and Chet Ballard. Oxford, UK: Blackwell Publishers.

Crescimanno, R. 1991. "The Cultivation of Critical Thinking: Some Tools and Techniques." *VCCA Journal* 6: 12–17.

Creswell, J. 1994. *Research Design: Qualitative and Quantitative Approaches.* Thousand Oaks, CA: Sage.

DeVita, C., and R. Mosher-Williams, ed. 2001. *Who Speaks for America's Children? The Role of Child Advocates in Public Policy.* Washington, D.C.: The Urban Institute Press.

DeWalt, K., and B. DeWalt. 2002. *Participant Observation, A Guide for Fieldworkers.* Walnut Creek, CA: Alta Mira Press.

Diamond, T. 1990. *Making Grey Gold: Narratives of Nursing Home Care*. Chicago, IL: University of Chicago Press.

Dreier, P. 2001. "How Will You Spend the 21st Century?" *American Sociological Association Footnotes:* 1–6. [On-line]. Available: http://www.asanet.org/footnotes (August 23, 2001).

DuBois, W. 1997. "A Model for Doing Applied Sociology: Insights and Strategies for an Activist Sociology." *Humanity and Society* 21 (1): 39–66.

Eckstein, R., R. Schoenike, and K. Delaney. 1995. "The Voice of Sociology: Obstacles to Teaching and Learning the Sociological Imagination." *Teaching Sociology* 23: 353–363.

Economic Policy Institute. 2001. "Poverty USA: The Working Poor." [On-line]. Available: http://www.usccb.org/cchd/poverty usa/ (February 1, 2004).

Ehrenreich, B. 2001. *Nickel and Dimed: On (Not) Getting By in America*. New York: Henry Holt and Company.

Ely, M. 1991. *Doing Qualitative Research: Circles within Circles*. London: The Falmer Press.

Emerson, R., R. Fretz, and L. Shaw. 1995. *Writing Ethnographic Fieldnotes*. Chicago, IL: University of Chicago Press.

Eyler, J., and D. Giles, Jr. 1999. *Where's the Learning in Service-Learning?* San Francisco, CA: Jossey-Bass Publishers.

Facione, P. 1998. "Critical Thinking: What It Is and Why It Counts." Pp. 1–16. Millbrae, CA: California Academic Press. [On-line]. Available: www.homestead.com/peoplelearn/criticalthinking.html.

Feagin. J. 2001. *Racist America: Roots, Current Realities, and Future Reparations*. New York: Routledge.

Feagin, J., and C. Feagin. 1990. *Social Problems: A Critical Power-Conflict Perspective*. 3rd ed. Englewood Cliffs, NJ: Prentice Hall.

Feagin, J., and H. Vera. 2001. *Liberation Sociology*. Cambridge, MA: Westview Press.

Fine, M., and L. Weis. 1998. *The Unknown City: The Lives of Poor and Working-Class Young Adults*. Boston, MA: Beacon Press.

Fowler, B. 1996. "Critical Thinking across the Curriculum Project." [On-line]. Available: http://www.kcmetro.cc.mo.uc/longview/ctac/definitins.htm (April 14, 2003).

Gaines, D. 1998. "Resurrecting Sociology as a Vocation." *Contemporary Sociology* 27: 454–457.

Gilbert, K., ed. 2001. *The Emotional Nature of Qualitative Research*. Boca Raton, FL: CRC Press.

Gillespie, D. 2003. "The Pedagogical Value of Teaching White Privilege through a Case Study." *Teaching Sociology* 31: 469–477.

Gitlin, T. 2003. *Letters to a Young Activist*. New York: Basic Books.

Goffman, E. 1959. *The Presentation of Self in Everyday Life*. New York: Anchor Books.

Goffman, E. 1961. *Asylums: Essays on the Social Structure of Mental Patients and Other Inmates*. Chicago, IL: Aldine Publishing Company.

Goldstein, A. 2003. "Practice vs. Privacy on Pelvic Exams." *Washington Post,* May 10, pp. A1–A9.

Goodall, H. L., Jr. 2000. *Writing the New Ethnography*. New York: Alta Mira Press.

Goodwin, G. 1997. "From Personal Troubles to Public Issues." Pp. 23–30 in *The Student's Companion to Sociology,* edited by Jon Gubbay, Chris Middleton, and Chet Ballard. Oxford, UK: Blackwell Publishers.

Grauerholz, L. 1999. "Creating and Teaching Writing-Intensive Courses." *Teaching Sociology* 27: 310–323.

Grauerholz, L., and S. Bouma-Holtrop. 2003. "Exploring Critical Sociological Thinking." *Teaching Sociology* 31: 485–496.

Green, C. 1999. "Liberal Learning versus Experiential Learning: False Polarities." Pp. 1–16 in *The Internship Handbook: Development and Administration of Internship Programs in Sociology,* edited by Richard Salem. Washington, D.C.: American Sociological Association.

Green, M. 1997. *Internship Success.* Chicago, IL: NTC/Contemporary Publishing Company.

Hamner, D. 2002. *Building Bridges: The Allyn and Bacon Student Guide to Service-Learning.* Boston, MA: Allyn and Bacon.

Hartley, J. 1994. "Case Studies in Organizational Research." Pp. 208–229 in *Qualitative Methods in Organizational Research: A Practical Guide,* edited by Catherine Cassell and Gillian Symon. Thousand Oaks, CA: Sage.

Hearn, J. 1998. "On Ambiguity, Contradiction and Paradox in Gendered Organizations." *Gender, Work and Organization* 5: 1–3.

Heaney, T. 1995. "Issues in Freirean Pedagogy." Pp. 13–14 [On-line]. Available: http://www.nl.edu/ace/Resources/Documents/FreireIssues.html (February 6, 2004).

Hironimus-Wendt, R., and L. Lovell-Troy. 1999. "Grounding Service-Learning in Social Theory." *Teaching Sociology* 27: 360–372.

Hochschild, A. 1983. *The Managed Heart: The Commercialization of Feeling.* Berkeley, CA: University of California.

Hollis, S. 2002. "Capturing the Experience: Transforming Community Service into Service-Learning." *Teaching Sociology* 30: 200–213.

Holyfield, L. 1997. "The Managed Heart by Arlie Hochschild." Pp. 242–243 in *The Student's Companion to Sociology,* edited by Jon Gubbay, Chris Middleton, and Chet Ballard. Oxford, UK: Blackwell Publishers.

Hondagneu-Sotelo, P., and S. Raskoff. 1994. "Community Service-Learning: Promises and Problems." *Teaching Sociology* 22: 248–254.

Horowitz, R. 1996. *Teen Mothers: Citizens or Dependents?* Chicago, IL: University of Chicago Press.

Huber, G., and A. VandeVen, ed. 1995. *Longitudinal Field Research Methods.* Thousand Oaks, CA: Sage.

Hylton, J., and J. Allen. 1993. "Setting Specific Purposes for Writing-to-Learn Assignments: Adapting the Dialogue Notebook for a Human Services Course." *Teaching Sociology* 21: 68–78.

Jary, D. 1997. "A Brief Guide to 'Difficult' Sociological Jargon and Some Working Resolutions." Pp. 174–181 in *The Student's Companion to Sociology,* edited by Jon Gubbay, Chris Middleton, and Chet Ballard. Oxford, UK: Blackwell Publishers.

Jary, D., and J. Jary. 1991. *The Harper Collins Dictionary of Sociology.* New York: Harper Perennial.

Johnson, A. 1997. *The Forest and the Trees: Sociology as Life, Practice and Promise.* Philadelphia, PA: Temple University Press.

Just Add Consciousness: A Guide to Social Activism. 2002. [On-line]. Available: http://www.oxfamamerica.org/publications/art1106.html (February 18, 2004).

Karis, T. 2002. "Pedagogical Approach to Race and Inequality: Strategies for Addressing Emotional Obstacles," an abstract. [On-line]. Available: http://www.uwm.edu/Dept/IRE/Events/Conferences/CriticalConnections/Abstracts/keownbomar4t4.html (May 27, 2003).

Kaufman, P. 1997. "Michael Jordan Meets C. Wright Mills: Illustrating the Sociological Imagination with Objects from Everyday Life." *Teaching Sociology* 25: 309–314.

Keats, D. 2000. *Interviewing, A Practical Guide for Students and Professionals.* Philadelphia, PA: Open University Press.

Kelly, C. 1997. "David Kolb, The Theory of Experiential Learning and ESL." *The Internet TESL Journal,* Vol. III, 9, September 1997. [On-line]. Available: http://iteslj.org/Articles/Kelly-Experential/ (July 2, 2001).

Kleinman, S. 1999. "Essaying the Personal: Making Sociological Stories Stick." Pp. 19–29 in *Qualitative Sociology as Everyday Life,* edited by Barry Glassner and Rosanna Hertz. Thousand Oaks, CA: Sage.

Kleinman, S., and M. Copp. 1993. *Emotions and Fieldwork.* Newbury Park, CA: Sage.

Kurland, D. 2000. "Steps in Critical Reading." [On-line]. Available: http://critical reading.com/step5.htm (March 12, 2004).

Kurtz, E., and K. Ketcham. 2002. *The Spirituality of Imperfection.* New York: Bantam.

LeCompte, M., and J. Schensul. 1999. *Analyzing & Interpreting Ethnographic Data.* Walnut Creek, CA: Alta Mira Press.

Leibrecht, D. 2001. "Commentary." *United States Catholic Conference.* [On-line]. Available: http://www.nccbuscc.org/cchd/povertyusa (January 8, 2001).

Lewis, T. 2004. "Service-Learning for Social Change? Lessons from a Liberal Arts College." *Teaching Sociology* 32: 94–108.

Liebow, E. 1993. *Tell Them Who I Am: The Lives of Homeless Women.* New York: Penguin Books.

Liebow, E. 1967. *Tally's Corner: A Study of Negro Streetcorner Men.* Boston, MA: Little, Brown.

Lindsay, P. 1996. "Group Project: A Design for a Theory-Testing Research Study." Pp. 245–253 in *Introductory Sociology Resource Manual,* 4th ed., edited by T. Amoloza and J. Sikora. Washington, D.C.: American Sociological Association.

Loeb, P. 1999. *Soul of a Citizen, Living with Conviction in a Cynical Time.* New York: St. Martin's Press.

Lofland, J., and L. Lofland. 1995. *Analyzing Social Settings: A Guide to Qualitative Observation.* Belmont, CA: Wadsworth Publishing Company.

Lynd, R. 1939. *Knowledge for What? The Place of Social Sciences in American Culture.* Princeton, NJ: Princeton University Press.

Lynd, H., and R. Lynd. 1929. *Middletown: A Study in American Culture.* New York: Harcourt Brace.

Macionis, J. 1999. *Sociology.* 7th ed. Upper Saddle River, NJ: Prentice Hall.

MacLeod, J. 1995. *Ain't No Makin' It: Aspirations and Attainment in a Low-Income Neighborhood.* Boulder, CO: Westview Press.

Martin, J. 2001. "Meta-Theoretical Controversies in Studying Organizational Culture." [On-line]. Available: http://gobi.stanford.edu/researchpapers/detail1.asp? Paper_No=1676 (July 22, 2002).

Marullo, S. 1999. "Sociology's Essential Role: Promoting Critical Analysis in Service-Learning." Pp. 11–27 in *Cultivating the Sociological Imagination: Concepts and Models for Service-Learning in Sociology,* edited by James Ostrow, Gary Hesser, and Sandra Enos. Washington, D.C.: American Association for Higher Education.

Marullo, S., and B. Edwards. 2000. "The Service-Learning Movement: Response to Troubled Times in Higher Education." *American Behavioral Scientist* 43: 746–912.

Mason, J. 2002. *Qualitative Researching.* Thousand Oaks, CA: Sage.

Maxwell, J. 1996. *Qualitative Research Design: An Interactive Approach.* Thousand Oaks, CA: Sage.

McIntosh, P. 1988. "White Privilege and Male Privilege: A Personal Account of Coming to See Correspondences through Work in Women's Studies." [On-line]. Available: http://www.utoronto.ca/acc/events/peggy1.htm (August 7, 2001).

McMillan, M. 1998. "What Are You Going to Do for Us?" *Humanity and Society* 22: 422–426.

Mead, G. H. 1934. *Mind, Self and Society.* Chicago, IL: University of Chicago Press.

Mickelson, R., ed. 2000. *Children on the Streets of the Americas: Homelessness, Education, and Globalization in the United States, Brazil, and Cuba.* New York: Routledge.

Miles, M., and A. M. Huberman. 1994. *Qualitative Data Analysis.* 2nd ed. Thousand Oaks, CA: Sage.

Miller, S. 1999. "Which 'Applied Sociology'?" *SSSP Newsletter* 30 (2): 21–22.

Mills, C. W. 1959. *The Sociological Imagination.* New York: Oxford University Press.

Mooney, L., and B. Edwards. 2001. "Experiential Learning in Sociology: Service-Learning and Other Community-Based Learning Initiatives." *Teaching Sociology* 29: 181–194.

Morrison, M. 2001. "School Is a Home for Children without One." *Washington Post* January 9, A03. [On-line]. Available: http://www.tjpappasschool.org/Washington Post2001Jan5.html (August 26, 2001).

National Center for Children in Poverty. 2003a. "Low-Income Children in the United States: A Brief Demographic Profile." [On-line]. Available: http://www.nccp.org/ycpf_03.htm (May 14, 2003).

National Center for Children in Poverty. 2003b. "Wake-Up America: Columbia University Study Shatters Stereotypes of Young Child Poverty." [On-line]. Available: http://www.nccp.org/wakeup.html (May 14, 2003).

National Service-Learning Clearinghouse. 1994. "Service-Learning Is . . ." [On-line]. Available: http://www.servicelearning.org/[Search_term=definitions+of+service+learning&m=all (March 12, 2004).

Neubeck, K., and D. Glasberg. 1996. *Sociology: A Critical Approach.* New York: McGraw-Hill.

Paul, R. 1990. *Critical Thinking: What Every Person Needs to Survive in a Rapidly Changing World.* Rohnert Park, CA: Center for Critical Thinking and Moral Critique.

Paul, R., and L. Elder. 2002. *Critical Thinking: Tools for Taking Charge of Your Professional and Personal Life.* Upper Saddle River, NJ: Financial Times, Prentice Hall.

Pettigrew, T. 1996. *Thinking Like a Social Scientist.* New York: Harper Collins Publishers.

Portland State University. "Definition of Community Based Learning at Portland State University." [On-line]. Available: http://www.cae.pdx.edu/ (March 12, 2004).

Potter, S., E. Caffrey, and E. Plante. 2003. "Integrating Service-Learning into the Research Methods Course." *Teaching Sociology* 31: 38–48.

Poverty Coalition UpDate. 2002. "Terminology." [On-line]. Available: http://www.poverty@infi.net (February 26, 2002).

Reinertsen, P., and G. DaCruz. 1996. "Using the Daily Newspaper and Journal Writing to Teach Large Introductory Sociology Classes." *Teaching Sociology* 24: 102–107.

Reinertsen, P., and M. Wells. 1993. "Dialogue Journals and Critical Thinking." *Teaching Sociology* 21: 182–186.

Reiman, J. 1996. *. . . And the Poor Get Prison.* Needham Heights, MA: Allyn and Bacon.

Ristock, J., and J. Pennell. 1996. *Community Research as Empowerment: Feminist Links, Postmodern Interruptions.* New York: Oxford Press.

Ritzer, G. 2000. *The McDonaldization of Society.* New Century Edition. Thousand Oaks, CA: Pine Forge Press.

Ritzer, G. 2002. "The Disenchanted Kingdom: George Ritzer on the Disappearance of Authentic American Culture." An interview by Derrick Jensen. *SUN* 318: 4–13.

Roschelle, A., J. Turpin, and R. Elias. 2000. "Who Learns from Service-Learning?" *American Behavioral Scientist* 43: 839–847.

Rossman, G., and S. Rallis. 1998. *Learning in the Field: An Introduction to Qualitative Research.* Thousand Oaks, CA: Sage.

Rubin, H., and I. Rubin. 1995. *Qualitative Interviewing: The Art of Hearing Data.* Thousand Oaks, CA: Sage.

Ruggiero, V. 1996. *A Guide to Sociological Thinking.* Thousand Oaks, CA: Sage.

Savage, D. 2003. "The Nation: Ranks of Poor are Thin at Top Colleges." *Los Angeles Times,* April 6, p. A34.

Schwalbe, M. 2001. *The Sociologically Examined Life: Pieces of the Conversation.* 2nd ed. Mountain View, CA: Mayfield Publishing Company.

Schwarz, J., and T. Volgy. 1992. *The Forgotten Americans.* New York: W. W. Norton & Co.

Scott, J. 2001. "In 90s Economy, Middle Class Stayed Put, Analysis Suggests." *New York Times.* [On-line]. Available: http://www.commondreams.org/headlines01/0831-03.htm (September 1, 2001).

Scriven, M., and R. Paul. "Defining Critical Thinking." [On-line]. Available: http://criticalthinking.org/university/univclass/Defing.html (June 27, 2001).

Shapiro, J. 2000. "From Sociological Illiteracy to Sociological Imagination." *The Chronicle of Higher Education.* March 31, A1. [On-line]. Available: http://chronicle.com/free/v46/i30/30a06801.htm (March 22, 2002).

Shaw, M. 1997. "From Public Issues to Personal Troubles." Pp. 31–38 in *The Student's Companion to Sociology,* edited by Jon Gubbay, Chris Middleton, and Chet Ballard, Oxford, UK: Blackwell Publishers.

Shiveley, J., and P. VanFossen. 2001. *Using Internet Primary Sources to Teach Critical Thinking Skills in Government, Economics, and Contemporary World Issues.* Westport, CT: Greenwood Press.

Sidel, R. 1996. *Keeping Women and Children Last: America's War on the Poor.* New York: Penguin Press.

Silver, I., and G. Perez. 1998. "Teaching Social Theory through Students' Participant Observation." *Teaching Sociology* 26: 347–353.

Smith, D. 1987. *The Everyday World as Problematic: A Feminist Sociology.* Boston, MA: Northeastern University Press.

Sohng, S. 1995. "Participatory Research and Community Organizing." [On-line]. Available: http://www.interwebtech.com/nsmnet/docs (May 15, 2002).

Spradley, J. 1980. *Participant Observation.* New York: Holt, Reinhart and Winston.

Stanton, T., and K. Ali. 1994. *The Experienced Hand: A Student Manual for Making the Most of an Internship.* 2nd ed. New York: Carroll.

Stevens, D., and M. VanNatta. 2002. "Teaching Critical Observation as a Sociological Tool." *Teaching Sociology* 30: 243–253.

Strand, K. 1999. "Sociology and Service-Learning: A Critical Look." Pp. 29–37 in *Cultivating the Sociological Imagination: Concepts and Models for Service-Learning in Sociology,* edited by James Ostrow, Gary Hesser, and Sandra Enos. Washington, D.C.: American Association for Higher Education.

Strand, K., S. Marullo, N. Cutforth, R. Stoecker, and P. Donohue. 2003. *Community-Based Research and Higher Education.* San Francisco, CA: Jossey-Bass.

Strauss, A. 1993. *Qualitative Analysis for Social Scientists.* New York: Cambridge University Press.

Strauss, A., and J. Corbin. 1997. *Grounded Theory in Practice.* Thousand Oaks, CA: Sage.

Sullins, P. 2001. "The Poverty Threshold: How the Government Defines Poverty in America." *Life Cycle Institute.* Washington, D.C.: The Catholic University of America.

Washington Post. 2003. "Insights into the Inmate Population." [On-line]. Available: http://washingtonpost.com/ac2/wp-dyn/A17684-2003May20 (May 24, 2003).

U.S. Census Bureau. 2002. "2001 Income and Poverty Statistics." *Almanac of Policy Issues.* September 24. [On-line]. Available: http://www.policyalmanac.org/social_welfare/archive/poverty_statistics (2001).

United Students against Sweatshops. 2004. [On-line]. Available: http://www.usanet.org (February 14, 2004).

Venkatesh, S. 2000. *American Project: The Rise and Fall of a Modern Ghetto.* Cambridge, MA: Harvard University Press.

Vogelgesang, L., and Rhoads, R. 2004. "Advancing a Broad Notion of Public Engagement: The Limitations of Contemporary Service-Learning." *Journal of College and Character* 2: 1–11.

Waddington, D. 1994. "Participant Observation." Pp. 107–122 in *Qualitative Methods in Organizational Research: A Practical Guide,* edited by Catherine Cassell and Gillian Symon. Thousand Oaks, CA: Sage.

Wagenaar, T. 1984. "Using Student Journals in Sociology Courses." *Teaching Sociology* 11: 419–437.

Ward, K., and L. Wolf-Wendel. 2000. "Community-Centered Service-Learning." *American Behavioral Scientist* 43: 767–780.

Whyte, W. F. 1943. *Street Corner Society: The Social Structure of an Italian Slum.* Chicago, IL: University of Chicago Press.

Williams, T. 1989. *The Cocaine Kids: The Inside Story of a Teenage Drug Ring.* Reading, MA: Addison-Wesley Publishing Co.

Wolcott, H. 1995. *The Art of Fieldwork.* Walnut Creek, CA: Alta Mira Press.

Yanay, N., and G. Shahar. 1998. "Professional Feelings as Emotional Labor." *Journal of Contemporary Ethnography* 27: 346–373.

Yin, R. 2003. *Case Study Research: Design and Methods.* Newbury Park, CA: Sage.

Young, I. 1990. *Justice and the Politics of Difference.* Princeton, NJ: Princeton University Press.

Author Index